VOLUME ONE:
TRADEMARKS & SYMBOLS OF THE WORLD

THE ALPHABET IN DESIGN

by Yasaburo Kuwayama

Rockport Publishers • Rockport, Massachusetts
Distributed by North Light Books
Cincinnati, Ohio

Copyright 1988 by Rockport Publishers

All rights reserved. No part of this
work may be reproduced in any form
without written permission of the
publisher.

Printed in Japan

First printing 1988

First published in the United States
of America in 1988 by:
Rockport Publishers
5 Smith Street
Rockport, MA 01966
TEL: (508)546-9590
FAX:(508)546-7141

For distribution by:
North Light, an imprint of
Writer's Digest Books
1507 Dana Avenue
Cincinnati, Ohio 45207

First published in Japan as
TRADEMARKS & SYMBOLS OF
THE WORLD by Kashiwashobo

Library of Congress cataloging in
publication data:

Kuwayama, Yasaburo
Trademarks & Symbols of the World:
The Alphabet In Design

ISBN: 4-7601-0451-8

Introductory Remarks

The contents of Trademark or Symbol data are as follows:

1)——Business Category
2)——Art Director
3)——Designer
4)——Client
5)——Year and Place Designed
6)——Color

All the works in this book were produced between 1970 and 1983.

Note

The marks and symbols contained in this book are the exclusive property of the designers and copyright holders. Some works are registered trademarks and are protected by law. All works represented in this book may not be reproduced or published without prior approval from the individual designers and copyright holders.

Contents

Introductory remarks ———————— 3

Notes ———————————————— 4

Contents ———————————————— 5

The World's Best Trademarks and Symbols —— 6

Classification and Arrangement ———— 7

Data ————————————————— 8

Artists and their works ———————— 9

A or A - like form ———————— 15

a or a - like form ———————— 25

B or B - like form ———————— 29

b or b - like form ———————— 35

C or C - like form ———————— 37

D or D - like form ———————— 48

d or d - like form ———————— 52

E or E - like form ———————— 54

e or e - like form ———————— 57

F or F - like form ———————— 59

f or f - like form ———————— 63

G or G - like form ———————— 65

g or g - like form ———————— 71

H or H - like form ———————— 72

h or h - like form ———————— 77

I or I - like form ———————— 78

i or i - like form ———————— 81

J or J - like form ———————— 83

j or j - like form ———————— 85

K or K - like form ———————— 86

k or k - like form ———————— 93

L or L - like form ———————— 94

M or M - like form ———————— 99

m or m - like form ———————— 107

N or N - like form ———————— 110

n or n - like form ———————— 114

O or O - like form ———————— 115

P or P - like form ———————— 118

p or p - like form ———————— 123

Q or Q - like form ———————— 126

R or R - like form ———————— 128

r or r - like form ———————— 132

S or S - like form ———————— 135

T or T - like form ———————— 147

t or t - like form ———————— 156

U or U - like form ———————— 157

u or u - like form ———————— 159

V or V - like form ———————— 160

W or W- like form ———————— 164

X or X - like form ———————— 168

Y or Y - like form ———————— 170

y or y - like form ———————— 172

Z or Z - like form ———————— 173

Index to Contained Works———————— 175

Index to Category of Business ———————— 204

Information about forthcoming editions(1985-91) ——— 207

The World's Best Trademarks and Symbols

This book is the revised version of the popular edition, "Trademarks and Symbols of the World", published in 1984. I have recomposed and selected 1,720 works derived from concrete forms, abstract forms, and symbols Contributions were made by 1,210 artists from 38 different countries. It can be said that these are the best representations in the world designed between 1970 and 1983. Moreover, they are thoughtful records that reveal the movements and trends of world visual design during the seventies and early eighties. This includes concepts and ideas in creating trademarks and symbols, as well as transitions and trends in their forms. I am more confident of this today eventhough 4 years have passed since this was originally published.

I was very surprised and happy to learn that many designers throughout the world have longed for such a book. Along with samples of their work, I have received about 200 letters of encouragement. In general, they said they were making good use of previous books in their work, and are looking forward to new good books on world graphic design (previous books include "Marks and Symbols 1, 2", which were published in 1972 in Japanese, English, and German). In order to meet designers' requests, this new edition is needed. The original version is quite bulky : A-4 size, 496 pages, and over 2kgs. It requires considerable stamina to use ! Because of the steady appreciation of the yen, it would be extremely costly for designers outside of Japan to obtain the original version. It would be a shame if a designer applied, and his or her works were presented in the book, but he or she were unable to obtain the book. Even though many students in the United States are using the original version, it is still prohibitively expensive for most students. That is why we've decided to transform the original version into two separate books : "The Alphabet in Design", and "Symbolical Design Elements ". I sincerely hope that these two volumes will be more accessible to designers and students throughout the world.

Now I feel as though a load has been taken off my shoulders...

January 1988 Yasaburo Kuwayama

Classification and Arrangement

The most outstanding feature of this book is that works have been classified and arranged according to form. Marks and symbols assume various forms depending on the individuality and feelings of the designers. I tried classifying and arranging the forms in such a way that anyone can look up a certain word just as easily as finding a word in a dictionary. If this method succeeds, anyone can find the form he is looking for, even if it is the first time he is using this book. Depending on the motif used in creating the form, the forms were classified into : (1) Alphabetical Forms ; (2) Concrete Forms ; (3) Abstract Forms ; and (4) Symbols, Numbers and Letters. Those which were alphabetical but expressed concrete forms, such as C being a bird (refer to page 41) and a fork and knife forming the letter H(651), were placed in the alphabet classification. Those which contained both concrete and abstract forms were placed in the concrete form classification. Those containing both an alphabet letter and a symbol or number were placed in the alphabet classification. When a work was related to two classifications, it was placed in the more significant classification.

1) Alphabet

The works were arranged in alphabetical order. When the letter forms were different for capital and small letters, they were classified separately. In the case of two-letter combinations, they were lined up in the AA, AB, AC order. Subsequent combinations of three or more letters were arranged in the same order as in a dictionary. Those with the same motif were divided according to similar forms and then lined up, from the simple to the complex.

2) Concrete Forms (Included in Visual Elements Design Source Book)

Human figures were placed into 3 different categories : Individual Human Forms, People, and Faces. Concrete forms were placed in the categories : Animals, Plants, Heavenly Bodies, Structures, and Tools. Human beings and things grouped together were arranged according to their numbers. Among them, they were lined up from simple forms to complex ones. Animals I includes wild animals, while Animals II includes livestock and domesticated animals.

They are classified according to form, which is different from a zoological classification. For instance, whales and dolphins are classified as fish, while the bat is classified as a bird and the snail as an insect.

3) Abstract Forms (Included in Visual Elements Design Source Book)

Abstract forms were placed in the 11 classifications of circles : forms which look like they are turning (including spirals), radial rays, those using circular arcs, triangles, squares, polygons with more than five sides, dots and collections of dots, straight lines, forms made by curves and three-dimensional expressions. In the case of two classification schemes, such as a circle inside a square, the form was placed in the classification of the outer shape (example : 1460). However, if it is part of a form, and when its impression is strong, then it was placed in that form. (example : 1450).

4) Symbols, Numbers and so on (Included in Visual Elements Design Source Book)

Symbols were divided into the categories : hearts, crosses, arrows, musical notes, etc. The numbers were lined up sequentially. In the case of repeating numbers, the simple ones were placed first. The Chinese characters and Japanese kana were placed in seven classifications.

Data

The following data has been attributed to each work : (1) Business category ; (2) Art Director ; (3) Designer ; (4) Client ; (5) Year Designed and Place (6) Color.

1) Business Category

The application form in English simply asked for "Category," so there were many cases in which the business category was not made clear because the designers wrote down only "mark" or "logotype". So that works could be selected according to business category, a business category index (pages 202-203) was established.

2) Art Director

Since this data depended on the application forms, the Art Director has not been included in cases where the space was left blank. When the work was the joint work of two people, the names of both were included.

3) Designer

There were a few that did not credit the designer. The application form had the name of the art director, but not the name of the designer. When the art director and the designer were the same person, the person's name was given in 2) and 3). When the designer was someone else, 2) and 3) were noted separately.

4) Client

The name of the client was coverted into Japanese only in those cases where the meaning was clear, but in the case of abbreviations, the Roman spelling was used. There were some that were proper nouns and had no meaning, and they were written in Japanese kana as much as possible.

5) Year and Place Designed

The "year designed" is noted according to the Christian calendar. There are some with two years noted, but this was due to joint designers submitting the same work separately and putting down different years, so that both years were noted. An R after the year denotes the year that the work was redesigned. Those with the * attached were designed prior to the 1970 -83 period but were judged necessary for inclu-sion because they had a major influence on works in the 1970-83 period.

"Place designed" was not noted on the application form, but this data was included since it can serve as a clue to judging in which area the work in being used. Since the place decided on the basis of the address of the person who submitted the work, there may be some place names which are not accurate. In the case of works from other countries, names of countries and cities that everyone knows were used. In the case of Japan, the prefecture names were used.

6) Color

In order to indicate the color as accurately as possible, the maker and color number were noted within parenthesis after the color name. There are some makers noted by their abbreviations as shown below. Those which do not have colors denoted had no decisive color.
Pantone／PMS＝Pantone Co. (U. S.)
DIC＝Dainippon Ink Chemical Industry (Tokyo)
TOYO CF＝Tokyo Ink Mfg. Co. (Tokyo)

Artists and Their Works

A

Abe Masahiro (Japan) 422,637,1614
Abe Toshirō (Japan) 806
Adrian, Frutiger (France) 1,148,175,719,1197, 1354,1511
Ajioka Shintarō (Japan) 1066,1327,1490
Akiyama Haruo (Japan) 852
Alexander, John M. (USA) 1231,1453
Alexiev, Christo (Bulgaria) 425
Allen, Steve (USA) 1046
Andrea, Marcello (Italy) 1250
Angone, Conrad E. (Los Angeles) 106,402, 1541
Aoki Hideki (Japan) 375,734,1174
Appelbaum + Curtis (New York) 1000,1167
Aguirre, Jose Luis (Roma) 663
Arape, Hugo (France) 261,443,893,1359,1520
Arima Tsuneo (Japan) 297
Asami Hiroshi (Japan) 216,265,1067
Ash, Stuart (Tronto) 187,257,400,764,945,1031, 1081,1227,1268,1645
Averink, Leen (France) 193,981

B

Baba Yūji (Japan) 266,1538
Baden, Carl (USA) 42
Ball, Gary (USA) 127,321
Baracz, Jolanta (Warsrawa) 61
Bartells, Dave (USA) 1400
Barton, J. (USA) 338
Bass, Joseph M. (Israel) 781,1084
Bass, Melanie (USA) 967
Bass, Saul (Los Angeles) 131,498,1513,1587
Baviera, Michael (Zürich) 807
Beltran, Felix (Mexico) 44,284,433,619,690,711, 858,937,996,1019,1088,1098,1267,1392,1420,1429, 1449,1484,1542,1543,1623,1627
Beltran, Orlando (Columbia) 43
Benavides, Elias Garcia (Spain) 142,453,1132, 1558
Benenti, Beppe (Italy) 439,511
Bertonceli, Matjaz (Yugoslavia) 227,419,871, 1314,1503
Binneweg, Herbert (Belgium) 415,1212
Bobn, Franktisek (Czechoslovakia) 385,399, 530,591,1659
Boggs, Joseph (USA) 575,930,1254,1579
Bohon, Ed (New York) 1114
Bondone, Di G. (Hong Kong) 1624
Bos, Ben (Amsterdam) 204,1562
Bowlend, Barbara (New York) 460
Brand, Chris (Brussels) 775,1452
Brown, Monica (USA) 622,632
Brown, Margaret S. (Canada) 238
Brod, Stan (USA) 167,566,622,632,964,1135,1292, 1676
Brown, John S. (Canada) 238,912,1077,1381
Bujatti, Madeleine (Austria) 117,694,1241
Bundzak, Bill (New York) 259,448,751,1613
Burcini, Francescco (Italy) 207,229,231,330, 398,430,580,705,732,846,934,952,1243,1564,1576
Burnazzi, Giovanni (Italy) 212,429,455,698,841, 1126,1149,1150,1151,1154,1219,1323,1334,1393,1527

C

Canales, Jorge (Mexico) 189,1303,1304,1309, 1483
Canovas, Eduardo A. (Argentine) 313,1281,

1422,1534,1591,1668
Capan, Edith (USA) 1105
Carlo, Marchionni (Italy) 1439
Carlo, Marearonni (Italy) 421,423
Carr, Frank (Mexico) 661
Carral, Jorge (Mexico) 1035
Carson, William (USA) 150,1475
Cartledge, Rick (Canada) 583,1110,1188,1221
Cartwright, Ted (Manchester) 248
Castro, Dicken (Columbia) 30,33,43,262,273,
281,607,1148,1172,1288,1504,1637
Cauduro, Joao Carlos (São Paulo) 28,317,
494,1039,1168,1206,1540
Ceccon, Vasco (Montreal) 434,1018
Centro Peril Disegno Ambientale (Italy) 362,
486,499,552,1234,1244,1436,1437
Chandler, Cliff (USA) 967
Chapman, Mike (USA) 601
Chavda, Jagdish (USA) 736
Chermayeff & Geismar Associates (USA)
205,620,621,702,774,1076,1347,1533,1568
Chōno Atsutaka (Japan) 527
Christensen, Carl (Oslo) 41
Churchward, Joseph (New Zealand) 368,752
Ciric, Milos (Beograd) 67,1678
Coll, Francisco Rendiles (Venezuela) 691
Connelly, Don (USA) 79,103,140,149,308,359,
644,645,918,925,957,1072,1217,1372,1463,1486
Cooke, Kenneth R. (New York) 595,1581
Coppola, Silvio (Milano) 4,8,706,867,870,1332,
1455,1508,1560,1582
Cordero, F. (New York) 1353
Cusik, Rick (USA) 318
Cutini, Rinaldo (Roma) 147,269,723,975,1083,
1497
Cutro, Associates, Inc (USA) 172,320,339,1204
Cutro, Ronald (USA) 172,320,339,1204
Crouwel, Wim (Amsterdam) 488

D

Dabinett, Peter (Ireland) 1464
Dacosta, Rey R. (Venezuela) 125,363,365,589,
596,875,1033,1078,1237,1238,1563
Davis, Don (USA) 122,128,130,526,610,741,904,
1301,1363,1507
Delany, George (USA) 788,1535,1561
Denis, Jan (London) 1054
Denzler, Fred E. (USA) 137,138,519,525,1338
Dheer, Sudarshan (Bombay) 188,215,557,821,
947,1112,1130,1239,1319,1320
Dicristo, Victor (USA) 1552
Dieter, Joe (USA) 536,745
Dieterich, Claude (Peru) 827,863,1512
Digianni, John (USA) 410,1157,1539
Dobson, Bruce (Los Angeles) 608
Doveri, Claudio (Milano) 598,1391
Dradi, Massimo (Milano) 477
Duschek (West Germany) 225,1396
Dvorsǎk, Ivan (Yugoslavia) 60,82,469,483,576,
709,726,1117,1367,1503,1505,1515,1516,1529

E

Eckersley, Richard (Ireland) 1181
Eckstein, Arthur (New York) 92,701,1091,1142,
1335
Edwards G. (Mexico) 192,647,1010
Eichenbaum, Ken (USA) 312,349,546,1191,1669
Engen Scott (USA) 468,810,933,971,1175,1182,

1257
Engle, Ray (Los Angeles) 139,504,959,1208,
1235,1360,1597,1602,1617
Engstrom, Ove (Sweden) 26,255,1049,1069,
1107,1407,1409,1423
Enomoto, Haruhilo (Japan) 1068
Erich, Unger (West Berlin) 1364
Emö, Tamás (Budapest) 327,384,1388,1389,
1459
Esteban, F. R. (USA) 58,237,337,367,1082,1120,
1349
Evans, Jack (USA) 35,78,95,133,143,166,233,450,
544,563,717,773,119,1121,1220,1377,1553,1578

F

Facchini, Umberto (Italy) 565
Fernandes, Rodrigo (Columbia) 63,291,292,
393,394,395,531,722,958,960,995,1058,1297,1315,
1358,1470,1491
Follis, John (Los Angeles) 198,417,515,928,1170,
1216,1412
Forbes, Everett (USA) 1554
Foster, Tony (Manchester) 136,211,248,642,643,
666,1161,1226,1228,1355,1482,1580,1612,1675
Frimkess, Lou (Los Angeles) 868,1316
Frozoni, A. G. (Mexico) 115,287,485
Frutiger, Adrian (France) 87,100,390,982
Fuhrman, Charies (USA) 1492
Fujii Hajime (Japan) 993
Fujii Kazuharu (Japan) 675,899,1012,1029,1269,
1417
Fujishige Teruo (Japan) 849,1435
Fukano Tadasu (Japan) 1635
Fukuda Masaaki (Japan) 538,823
Fukuda Shigeo (Japan) 754,1318,1418,1456
Furhoff, Eva-Lotta (Sweden) 1407
Furumura Osamu (Japan) 413
Furuta Masaki (Japan) 447
Furuta Osamu (Japan) 89

G

Gale, Robert A. (New York) 252,1047
Galli, Pietro (Italy) 85,354,1097,1201
Games, Abram (London) 1361
Garamond, Jacques N. (France) 59,742
Garnier, Florent (Lyon) 27,279,1325,1556
Gassner, Christof (Frankfurt) 521
Gault, Joe (Toronto) 1431
Gayton, silvio (USA) 277,348,382,558,611,660,
1115
Gersin, Robert P. (New York) 221,623,1038,
1056,1603
Gianninoto, Associates Inc. (New York) 410,
1157,1539
Gibbs, David (USA) 478
Giovanni, Martelossi (Milano) 1544
Gips, Philip (New York) 62,105,600,1053,1192,
1523
Glaser, Miton (New York) 316,358,369,707,
1536,1584
Gomes-Casallas, Gustavo (Columbia) 63,291,
292,393,394,395,531,710,722,958,960,995,1058,1210,
1297,1315,1358,1470,1491
Gotō Toshio (Japan) 505
Gotti, Paolo (Italy) 1406
Gottschalk+Ash, International (Toronto) 187,
257,400,764,945,1031,1081,1200,1227,1268,1645
Gottschalk, Fritz (Toronto) 257

Graham, Diana (New York) 1198,1593
Gustavsson, Torgny (Sweden) 1107,1423
Gustus, Dawn (USA) 771
Gutierrez, Abner (New York) 623

H

Hackett, Dave (USA) 1191
Hagiwara Nobuyuki (Japan) 548
Hamada Kazufumi (Japan)
Harder, Rolf (Montreal) 319,372,1036,1183
Hargenhoffer, Robert (USA) 101,151,355,626,
822,910,972,1262,1306,1351,1532
Harrington, Damien (Ireland) 683,897,1317,1639
Hartig, Karl (New York) 1027
Hartzheim, Hans (Hague) 574
Hasegawa Sumio (Japan) 446,814,1427
Hatakeyama Satoshi (Japan) 907
Healey, Gavin (London) 559,811,866
Henrion, FHK (London) 885,1054
Harb, Yagur and Assoc. (Los Angeles) 1513,
1587
Hergenrother, Walter (Italy) 88,98,222,271,396,
436,508,550,704,844,1419
Herold, Michael (West Germany) 121,144,633,
662,813,830,873,886,978,1003,1310,1313,1460,1518,
1573,1642,1673
Hirata Akira (Japan) 11,31,160,380,553,592,748,
763,845,1245,1537,1598
Hirose Ken'ichi (Japan) 37,761,894,909,1607
Hirotani Ryüji (Japan) 1171
Hoashi Jitsuo (NewYork) 793,1263
Hoashi Studio (New York) 1263,2070
Hochuli, Jost (Switzerland) 883,1034,1124,1133,
1193,1276
Hoed, Rout Van Den (USA) 646
Hollender, Jan (Poland) 699,1109
Hollick, Kenneth (London) 241,244,403,539,615,
737,778,1524
Hughes, Edward (USA) 82,240,578,604,1145,
1165,1339,1374,1411
Hunt, Wayne (Los Angeles) 198,928

I

Ibov, Paul (Belguim) 13,76,97,168,206,376,440,
449,497,590,627,655,697,708,809,851,881,919,926,
965,968,979,1169,1176,1242,1289,1343,1394,1447,
1522,1565,1571,1574,1643,1644
Igarashi Takenobu (Japan) 265,825,1328,1408,
1438,1440,1674
Iguchi Yasuhisa (Japan) 791,991,1330,1344,1345,
1474
Iijima Moriyoshi (Japan) 584
Ikeda Shin (Japan) 22,577
Ikeda Norio (Japan) 688
Ikemoto Hiroko (Japan) 377
Ikola, Gale William (USA) 169,190,685,1026,
1400,1500
Iliprandi, Giancarlo (Milano) 1189,1202,1397
Inamoto Yukio (Japan) 46
Inouchi Hiroyasu (Japan) 612
Inoue Takahiro (Japan) 1190
Iseya Hiroshi (Japan) 1187,1660
Ishida Mitsuo (Japan) 543,806,902,1667
Ishii Masaaki (Japan) 1655
Ishikawa Tadashi (Japan) 1061,1395
Ishikawa Teruo (Japan) 796
Istvan, Morocz (Budapest) 618
Istvan, Szekeres (Budapest) 129,191,541,653,

712,799,908,985,1113,1215,1273,1569
Isuzu Jidōsya （Japan） 682,1230
Itō Jutarō （Japan） 999
Itō Katsuichi （Japan） 356,414,617,815,912
Itō Seika （Japan） 715
Ivanov, Assen （Bulgaria） 1457
Ivorsohk, Azer Khosrovi （New York） 243,
1499

J
Jaggie, Fredy （Toronto） 257
Jasinski, Jarostaw （Warszawa） 61,489,528,
1166,1595
Jaszczuk, Woiciech （Poland） 1109
Jensik, Jerome （Los Angeles） 1235
Jinbo Yoneo （Japan） 641
Joe, Alvin （USA） 1140
Johansson, Ingvar （Sweden） 255,1069
Joynes, Kathleen Trainor （USA） 200

K
Kalderon, Asher （Israel） 743,891,912,981,1041
Kanai Kazuo （Japan） 1139,1214
Kamata Tsuneyo （Japan） 1016
Kaneko Ken'ichi （Japan） 1037
Kaneko Kenji （Japan） 676
Kanise Yukio （Japan） 250,803,1199,1209
Kantscheff, Stephan （Bulgaria） 72,73,109,132,
134,135,182,202,203,246,256,293,309,310,311,326,
328,343,353,393,416,442,444,506,532,534,535,537,
594,625,790,817,826,839,900,942,943,955,963,983,
1001,1062,1074,1159,1160,1164,1173,1177,1380,1414,
1448,1478,1495,1496,1501,1633,1650,1651,1662,1672
Karlsson, Kurt （Sweden） 1409
Karoly, Lederer （Budapest） 1469
Katsube Tadamasa （Japan） 86,714,1136,1375,
1433
Katsuoka Shigeo （Japan） 39,216,471,510,716,
944,988,1007,1021,1022,1067,1100,1190,1271
Kawachi Yūji （Japan） 941
Kawamoto Nagato （Japan） 766,1550
Kawarabayashi Yūji （Japan） 547
Kimura Ikuya （Japan） 731,859,1090,1155,1246
Kishimoto Kazuo （Japan） 65,551,606
Kishimoto Yoshihiro （Japan） 48,715,747
Kleiner, T. （Israel） 1041
Klose, Stanton （USA） 1103
Kneebone, Peter （Paris） 587
Kobayashi Shigeji （Japan） 382,792,1286,1646
Koga Yukio （Japan） 1059
Komatsubara Masamitsu （Japan） 487
Kondō Mariko （Japan） 796
Kopp, Warner （USA） 829
Korten, Manfred （West Germany） 116,408,554,
718,1044,1387,1517
Koseki Shirō （Japan） 112
Kovář, Stanislav （Praha） 247,1378
Koyoda Fumio （Japan） 34,80,163,346,523,548,
569,882,992,994,1005,1300
Kramer, Burton （Toronto） 118,126,186,196,288,
289,329,388,572,573,629,630,639,820,1085,1137,
1194,1282,1294,1295,1340,1431,1462,1640,1641
Krol Stan （London） 1636
Ku, Jennings （Hong Kong） 686
Kudō Tsuyokatsu （Japan） 673
Kuginuki Hiromi （Japan） 1598
Kündig, Hans （Sweden） 603,661,878,1125,1382
Kurobe Yoshihiko （Japan） 15

Kutač, Vincenc （Praha） 247
Kuwabara Akiyoshi （Japan） 818,1052
Kuwayama Yasaburō （Japan） 167,503,586,671,
678,804,838,887,921,922,939,950,1051,1064,1096,
1162,1196,1442,1601,1615
Kyōi Kiyoshi （Japan） 152,1654

L
Lao, Ling Chay Y. （Philippines） 1346
Larsen, Kenneth （USA） 949
Larsen, Tim （USA） 195,1005
Larsen, Gum （Sweden） 616,923
Larson, Kerstin （Sweden） 923
Lebowitz, Mo （New York） 304,1123
Lega, Jaime Gutierrez （Columbia） 496,1369
Lehfeld, Ernest （Mexico） 40,94,184,391,392,411,
412,421,428,656,1329
Leidel, Mike （USA） 735
Leigh, David （New York） 460,461,522,599
Lendvai, Laszlo （Budapest） 464
Leon, Javier De （Mexico） 1284
Lesniewicz, Terry （USA） 107,173,185,220,373,
405,567,652,784,951,1390,1619
Leufert, Gerd （Venezuela） 93,245,938,1336,
1370,1559
Lewis, S. （New York） 345
Lienhart, James （Chicago） 75,232,258,305,314,
470,549,657,805,1101,1102,1383,1386,1577,1670
Lifton, Diana （USA） 454
Lim, Steve （New York） 865
Lindholm, Sture （Sweden） 665
Lizardi, Ben （USA） 1360
Lohman, H. W. （Netherlands） 1589
Lovell, Brian （USA） 1163
Luigi, Miani （Milano） 209,540,1253,1494

M
Mabry, Micheal （USA） 177
Mabuchi Tetsuharu （Japan） 516,888
Maetani Katsumi （Japan） 1290
Maki Katsuhiko （Japan） 112
Malerba, Carlo （Italy） 16,374,490,597,892,1275,
1324,1476,1629
Mann, Kazimieiz （Poland） 528,1119,1595
Manzen Hiroshi （Japan） 20,302,315,1337
Marc, Burkhalter （Switzerland） 501,1506
Martino, Ludovico Antonio （São Paulo） 28,
317,494,1039,1168,1206,1540
Masubuchi Ikuo （Japan） 487,586,1663
Masubuchi Kuniharu （Japan） 1178
Matsunaga Shin （Japan） 51,89,1079
Maurer, Hansueli （Zürich） 835
Mazzara, Maria （USA） 347,466,1014
McGinnis, George （New York） 656,699,895,
1549
McKinney, Debbie （USA） 735,920
Medina, Fernando （Madrid） 23,114,351,840,862
Meyer, Rudi （France） 197,1600,1671
Michaw, Roland （France） 197,1600
Michaw, Yvette （France） 197,1600
Milani, Armando （Milano） 45,56,57,194,260,901,
916,1011,1092,1203,1207,1252,1413,1421,1531,1666
Milani, Maurizio （Milano） 57,260,299,901,916,
1011,1092,1252,1413,1421,1514,1531,1666
Miller, Allen W. （USA） 71,307,383,568,1461
Misaki Harumasa （Japan） 1015
Mitani Yutaka （Japan） 333,635
Mitnick, Joel （New York） 1152

Miyanaga Iwao （Japan） 678,921
Miyasaka Katsumi （Japan） 815
Mizuno Kōichi （Japan） 509,533
Mizuno Shinsaku （Japan） 687
Mjos, Rockford （USA） 180,235
Mohr, Gunter （USA） 127
Morfos, Diseno S. C. （Mexico） 146,183,475,
725,880,1104,1285,1432
Moltke, Adam （Denmark） 218,518,787,1266,1352
Momayez, Morteza （Tehran） 613
Mori Kōji （Japan） 31,80,748,750,763,845,1598
Mori Yoshinori （Japan） 614
Morioka Yoshimichi （Japan） 1583
Morishita Kageyoshi （Japan） 1025
Moroboshi Kanju （Japan） 713
Mosco, Charles M. （New York） 560
Motter, Othmar （Austria） 124,144,155,159,165,
174,181,224,230,366,495,564,609,729,746,755,832,
834,836,837,1279,1299,1307,1362,1376,1458,1545,
1546,1547,1606
Muller, Jean-Claude （USA） 417,482,758,1412,
1416,1485
Munar, Nestor （Columbia） 43
Murgatroyd, Keith （London） 136,213,642,643,
666,876,1161,1228,1467,1482,1580,1628
Murphy, Harry （USA） 480,636,728,772,798,1103,
1233,1605

N
Nagai Kazumasa （Japan） 2,3,12,756,783,1261,
1404,1638,1647
Nagaishi Shigenobu （Japan） 1434,1443
Nagao Akinori （Japan） 1408
Nagata Katsumi （Japan） 586,1096
Nakajima Akiteru （Japan） 14,64,1498
Nakajima Takeshi （Japan） 210
Nakano Yoshiaki （Japan） 533
Nakatani Kyōji （Japan） 1079
Nakayama Tajiro （Japan） 1405,1567
Nakazawa Hidemi （Japan） 749
Naitō Junko （Japan） 11
Nambu Toshiyasu （Japan） 581
Naumov, Petar （Bulgaria） 1555
Nava, R. （Italy） 486,499,552,1184,1234,1244,1436,
1437
Navarre, Al （USA） 107,173,185,220,373,405,652,
784,951,1390,1619
Nelson, Carl （USA） 1596
Nemes, Júlis （Hungary） 476,1006
Netziel, Kurt （Sweden） 665
Neumann, Robert L （USA） 720
Neumeier, Marty （USA） 74,120,253,306,457,1618
Nichols, Don （New York） 104,352,479,593
Niinomi Syunji （Japan） 228,516,888,909
Nikolov, Nikola （Bulgaria） 77,90,300,344,370,
401,677,800,1403
Nishida Naoko （Japan） 845
Nishino Hiroshi （Japan） 673
Nishizawa Masayuki （Japan） 1660
Niitsuma Ishine （Japan） 1405
Noda Tetsuo （Japan） 1030,1042,1063
Novarese, Aldo （Italy） 491
Nozaki Toshinori （Japan） 986

O
Oda Katsunori （Japan） 1270
Ogawa Osamu （Japan） 208,797,941,993
Ogawa Tadahiko （Japan） 898

Artists and their Works

Ogura Hisako （Japan）53
Ogura Michio （Japan）340,608,1519
Ohmer, Thomas （Los Angeles）158,285,500,
608,684,780,868,1316,1371,1426
Oike Kimio （Japan）1025
Oka Yasumasa （Japan）234,1040
Okada Ichirô （Japan）1648
Okazawa Gô （Japan）654
Okuda Hiroyuki （Japan）239,948
Oohashira Kimito （Japan）1225
Ooki Kigen （Japan）456
Oomori Shigeshi （Japan）1247,1356,1398
Oonishi Sôgen （Japan）760,768,1585
Oono Kazuo （Japan）119,520,924,1677
Oota Tetsuya （Japan）249,1032,1373,1488
Ootaka Takeshi （Japan）1087,1401
Ortiz, Jose Luis （Spain）1106
Osti, Maurizio （Italy）1406

P

Paniagua, Santos （Milwaukee）69
Patil, Neelkamal （India）821,1100
Patil, Prakash （Bombay）556
Pecareff, Nicolai （Bulgaria）1526,1555
Pehoski, Dennis （USA）1179
Penniman, Ed （USA）141,164,770,864,1048,1060,
1122,1487
Peter, Chistensen （Switzerland）561,1506,1548
Petrov, Velizar （Bulgaria）157,913,946,966,1249,
1454,1465,1630
Pettersen, Tor （London）99
Pham-Phu, Oanh （München）10,171,420,508,
562,664,872,1004,1195,1211,1236,1293,1298,1608
Plati, Kathie （USA）920
Ponce, Alfonso Capetillo （Mexico）656
Potocki, James （Los Angeles）1170,1216
Pusva's, Lasziô （Budapest）808
PVDI （Brasil）52,272,341,371,1248,1626,1665

Q

Quon, Mike （New York）324,345,406,481,739,
805,874,884,1153,1185,1186,1353

R

Rathousky, Jiri （Czechoslovakia）1144,1428,
1679
Redaelli, Guido （Milano）9,161,209,540
Resser, Coutney （Los Angeles）780
Remington, R. Roger （New York）102,263,
437,1071,1095,1118,1341
Reuter, Linda （USA）176
Rey, Ricardo （Puerto Rico）1129,1178
Reynolds, Kip （USA）110
Richards, Micheal （USA）84,177,956,1525
Richards, Ron （Canada）389,1089,1566
Rion, Fernando （Mexico）96,296,322,378,693,
730,861,879,915,1035,1043,1127,1218,1528
Robin, Randi （USA）110,604,607
Roch, Ernst （Montreal）264,456,649
Roland, Carlos （Barcelona）178,517
Romani, G. （Italy）1234,1436,1437,1834
Rubin, David （Los Angeles）324
Ruiz, Guillermo Gonzales （Buenos Aires）
70,268,513,679,1143,1232
Russell, Micheal J. （London）459,1055
Ruuska, Pentti （Finland）1342

S

Saijô Hiroyasu （Japan）334,1481
Saitô Sôichi （Japan）617
Saitô Yoshiharu （Japan）160
Sakado Hideko （Japan）1061,1395
Sakamoto Kenji （Japan）1433
Sakata Eiko （Japan）1247,1356,1398
Saks, Arnold （Los Angeles）1027,1472
Sakuma Tôru （Japan）1028
Salaroli, Sergio （Roma）753
Salas, Ricardo （Mexico）1284
Saldan, Halmut （Amsterdam）236,914
Sanada Akira （Japan）1326
Santamarina, Elias （Spain）987,1080,1355
Santamarina, José （Spain）156,267,987,1080,
1116,1365
Santis, Alfrendo De （Roma）49,335,463,545,
643,889,896,1205,1446,1510
Sara, Erno （Budapest）444,476,618,808,1006,
1409
Sasaki Shin （Japan）974,1424
Sasaki Takao （Japan）635
Satake Yasunori （Japan）34
Satô Shigeru （Japan）1068
Satô Tamami （Japan）543,902
Satô U. G. （Japan）295
Satô Yutaka （Japan）961,1399,1408,1471,1661
Scheur, Hans E. （West Germany）842,1259,
1368
Schillemans, A. G. （Amsterdam）201,219,1008,
1274
Schlosser, Cyril John （USA）301,409,669,672,
1357
Schneider, Werner （West Germany）980
Schumacher, Johann （New York）1056
Scott, Eric （New York）595
Selame, Joe （USA）109,782,940,1251,1350,1620
Selame, Design Group （USA）108,782,940,
1251,1350,1620
Sellzer, Carl （Los Angeles）158,500,684
Serna, Fernando De La （Mexico）1304
Sewell, Sylvia （London）459,1055
Sganzerla, Angelo （Milano）199,689,936,1272,
1301
Shakespear, Los （Buenos Aires）290,1057,
1147,1632
Shakespear, Raul （Buenos Aires）68,927,1551
Shakespear, Ronald （Buenos Aires）68,927,
1551
Shakespear, Design Studio （Buenos Aires）
68,927,1551
Shelden, Steve （USA）464,588,1131,1188,1575
Shibata Shigetoshi （Japan）397
Shibuya Hiroshi （Japan）505
Shima Takahiro （Japan）7
Shimokawa Masatoshi （Japan）361
Shimoyama Tsutomu （Japan）769
Shinohara Eita （Japan）50,647,953,962,989
Shirahama Kumi （Japan）1442
Skalar, Judita （Yugoslavia）1128,1451
Skalar, Peter （Yugoslavia）145
Sliwka, Karol （Poland）1094
Snellenberg, Evert （Amsterdam）204
Soffentini, D. （Italy）486,499,552,1184,1234,1244,
1436,1437
Sommese, Lanny （USA）507,648,651,855,877,
977
Sonderman, Joe （USA）1510,1592

Sönmez, Selahattin （Istanbul）91,360,721,724,
779,1477
Sonohara Toshio （Japan）1002
Sood, Ashok （Bombay）188
Soyster & Ohren Schall, Inc （USA）164
Spaulding, Denise （USA）294,404,824,1180,1224,
1445
Spohn, Jürgen （West Berlin）720
Sposari, Jorge （Argentine）323,427,976,1333
Staehelin, Georg （Zürich）55,816
Stankowski, Anton （West Germany）225,650,
668
Starr, Thomas （New York）474,765
Stein, Doris （USA）546
Steiner, Henry （Hong Kong）331,634,686,738,
1410,1624
Stoddard, Joe （Los Angeles）515
Stone, Gina （New York）1523
Strempel, Rainer （West Germany）458,472
Sugaya Sadao （Japan）276,1108
Sugaya Takeo （Japan）210,1616
Suzuki Hideto （Japan）447
Suzumori Yasunori （Japan）869
Swatek, Randall （USA）765
Swensen, Bill （USA）84
Swisher, Bob （USA）303,325,1009,1013,1105,1287

T

Tada Hiroshi （Japan）214,592,1245,1537
Taipei Creative Center （Taiwan）32
Tajima Kazuo （Japan）6,833,1016,1017
Takahara Shin'ichi （Japan）25,418,501
Takahashi Hideshi （Japan）527
Takahashi Minoru （Japan）21,275,905,1023
Takahashi Toshiaki （Japan）819,1291
Takakita Yukihisa （Japan）789,1479
Takashima Kenzô （Japan）1586
Takei Kôji （Los Angeles）285,1426
Takatomo Tomoko （Japan）53
Taki Masami （Japan）692
Tamamoto Kazuho （Japan）997
Tami Yoshikatsu （Japan）38,786,1258
Tanabe Masakazu （Japan）19,1205,1622
Tanaka Ikkô （Japan）66,249,251,744,831
Tanaka Jôji （Japan）1521
Tanaka Kazuo （Japan）445,681,848,1158,1204,
1278
Tastan, Burhan （Istanbul）350,514
Tateshi Tetsuhiro （Japan）1667
Taylor, Pat （USA）424,1213
Tchakarov, Stefan （Bulgaria）801,1634
Tellez, Francisco （Mexico）441
Terao Hiro （Japan）492,680
Tissi, Rosmarie （Zürich）54,200,570,653,1444
Toida Hiroshi （Japan）24,29,776
Topczewski, Mark （USA）312,349
Torigoe Syûji （Japan）670,998,1425
Tscherny, George （New York）123,226,493,
1331,1469,1609,1625
Turlakova, Eleonora （Bulgaria）425
Turner, Philip J. （Great Britain）1348
Tunner, Tracy （New York）439,555

U

Ubertazzi, A. （Italy）486,499,522,547,1184,1234,
1244,1436,1437
Ueda Akisato （Japan）18,36,46,47,387,547,612,
654,659,777,911,935,1222,1260,1402,1653

Ullenberg, Frances (USA) 214,312,349
Ulmer, Peter G. (Swizerland) 170,223,1599
Umezawa Hisahiro (Japan) 828
Unigraphics, Inc (USA) 544
Urata Meiko (Japan) 1028
Urban, Dieter (Brusseis) 278,452,624,954,984

V

Van Der Wal, Julien (Genéve) 298,660,906
Vandame, Michel (Columbia) 394
Vanderbyl Michael (San Francisco) 286,1622
Vellvé, Tomás (Barcelona) 357,703
Vera, Joe (Mexico) 381,441,542,1099,1106
Vitale, Ettore (Roma) 280,435,451,657,1256,1321,
  1450,1530
Vogt, Armin (Switzerland) 154,438,471,582

W

Wada Yasuo (Japan) 1604
Waibl, Heinz (Milano) 556,1075,1588
Walczak, Jacek (Warszawa) 489
Walczak, Tytus (Warszawa) 379,529,1305,1415
Wallen, Arvid (USA) 970
Watanabe Kôichi (Japan) 17,270,638,762,767,
  859,929,990,1020,1024,1070,1430,1441
Watanabe Kunio (Japan) 767
Weber, Hans (Zürich) 835
Weiss, Jack (USA) 110,454,667
Wellner, Peter (Budapest) 113
Wenn, Herbert (West Germany) 462,512,640,
  757,1590,1611
Whalen, Mike (USA) 527
White, Ken (Los Angeles) 1208
Wiens, Duane (USA) 42,970
Wildbur, Peter (London) 1086
Williams, Douglan (USA) 1475
Willis, Robert L. (USA) 242,336
Wittosch, Richard (USA) 153,332,386,740,1240
Wolf, Robert (New York) 1581
Woo, Calvin (USA) 81,524,579
Woo, Eric (USA) 81
Wunderlich, Gert (East Germany) 473
Wunderlich, Sonja (East Germany) 467,794,
  890
Wutke, Manfred (West Germany) 217,658,932,
  1229,1308

Y

Yakult Cosmetics (Japan) 48
Yeager, Richard (USA) 254,601
Yamada Yonefusa (Japan) 974
Yamaguchi Iwao (Japan) 1652
Yamaguchi Shigô (Japan) 447,802,809,1521,
  1571
Yamamoto Tatsuhito (Japan) 1147
Yamao Hidemichi (Japan) 502,631,1050,1658
Yano Harukata (Japan) 680
Yanagida Hironobu (Japan) 602
Yasuda Katsuhiko (Japan) 414
Yoguchi Takao (Japan) 1666
Yoneda Shizuo (Japan) 990,1441
Yoshida Makoto (Japan) 162,484,585,654,903,
  1311,1312
Yoshida Yoshihiro (Japan) 795,1073
Yoshimura Hajime (Japan) 679
Yoshinaga Katsuyoshi (Japan) 1045
Yoshinobu Takaaki (Japan) 785,812
Young, Don (USA) 5,432,628,1103

Yu-Lin, Kao (Taipei) 32,157,973,1296,1384,1489

Z

Zahor, Bruce D. (New York) 111,283,1152
Zamparelli, Mario (USA) 931
Zapata, Eduardo (Mexico) 1043,1111
Zapf, Hermann (West Germany) 733,879
Zen Kinya (Japan) 785
Zetterborg, Bror B. (Helsinki) 1277
Zoulamis, Chris (New York)

1

2

3

4

5

A

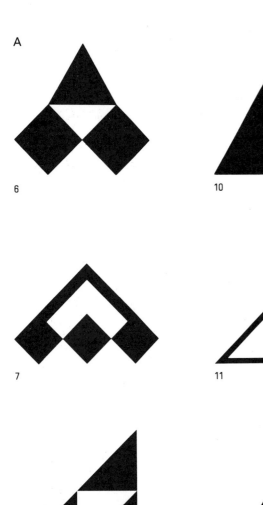

6

10

14

7

11

15

8

12

16

9

13

17

18

22

26

19

23

27

20

24

28

21

25

29

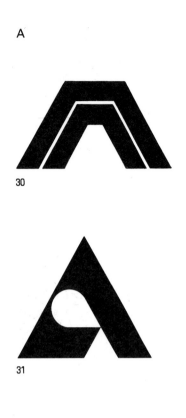

30

31

34

35

38

39

32

36

40

33

37

41

42

46

50

43

47

51

44

48

52

45

49

53

54

58

62

55

59

63

56

60

64

57

61

65

66

70

74

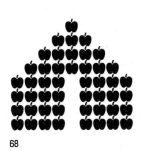

67

71

75

68

72

76

69

73

77

78

82

86

79

83

87

80

84

88

81

85

89

90

94

98

91

95

99

92

96

100

93

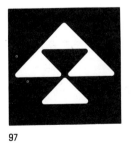

97

101

102

106

110

103

107

111

104

108

112

105

109

113

114

119

120

115

117

121

116

118

122

123

127

131

124

128

132

125

129

133

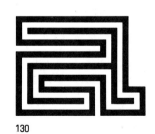

126

130

134

135

139

143

136

140

144

137

141

145

138

142

146

147

151

155

148

152

156

149

153

157

150

154

158

159

160

161

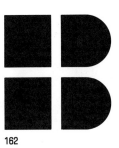

162

163

B

164

168

172

165

169

173

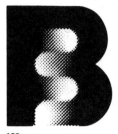

166

170

174

167

171

175

176

180

184

177

181

185

178

182

186

179

183

187

188

192

196

189

193

197

190

194

198

191

195

199

200

204

208

201

205

209

202

206

210

203

207

211

B

212

216

220

213

217

221

214

218

222

215

219

223

34

200

204

208

201

205

209

202

206

210

203

207

211

B

212

216

220

213

217

221

214

218

222

215

219

223

224

229

230

225

227

231

226

228

232

233

237

241

234

238

242

235

239

243

236

240

244

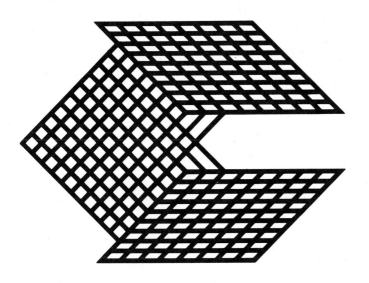

245

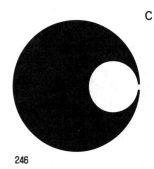

246

247

248

249

C

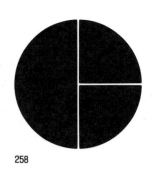

250

254

258

251

255

259

252

256

260

253

257

261

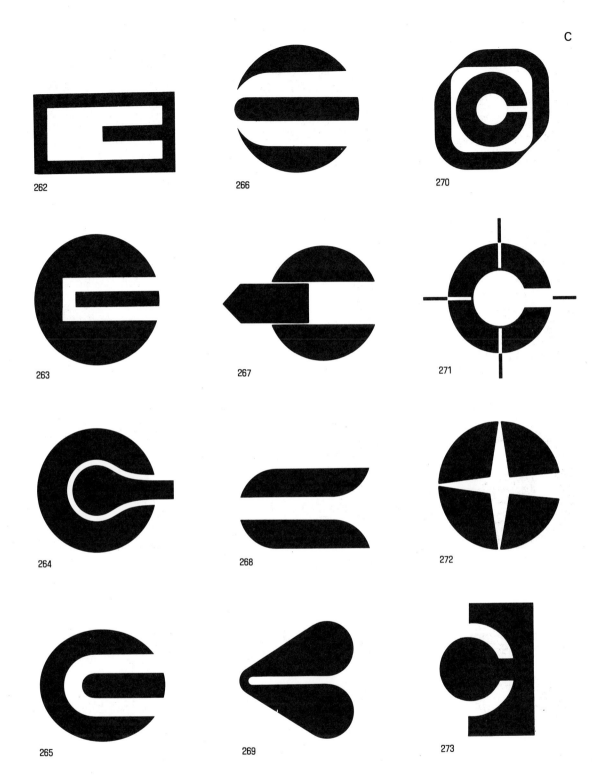

262

266

270

263

267

271

264

268

272

265

269

273

C

274

275

276

277

278

279

280

281

282

283

284

285

40

286

287

288

289

290

291

292

293

294

295

296

297

C

298

302

306

299

303

307

300

304

308

301

305

309

310

314

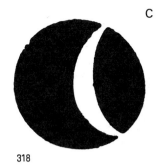

318

311

315

319

312

316

320

313

317

321

C

322

326

330

323

327

331

324

328

332

325

329

333

334

338

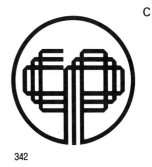

342

335

339

343

336

340

344

337

341

345

C

346

350

354

347

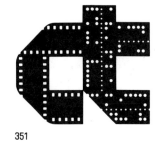

351

355

348

352

356

349

353

357

358

362

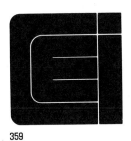

366

359

363

367

360

364

368

361

365

369

D

370

371

372

373

374

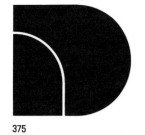

375

379

383

376

380

384

377

381

385

378

382

386

D

387

391

395

388

392

396

389

393

397

390

394

398

399

403

407

400

404

408

401

405

409

402

406

410

411

412

415

413

416

418

414

417

419

420

421

422

423

424

425

426

427

428

429

430

431

E

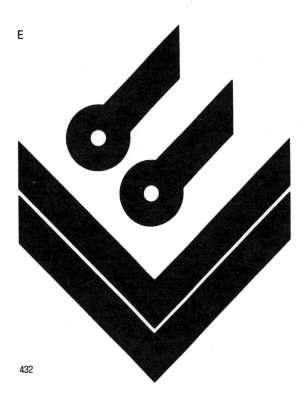

432

433

434

435

436

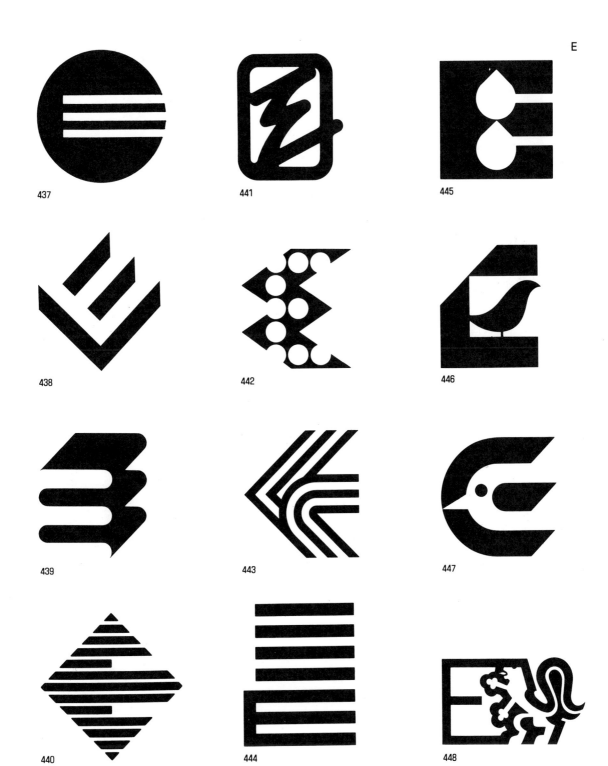

437

441

445

438

442

446

439

443

447

440

444

448

E

449

457

450

454

458

451

455

459

452

456

460

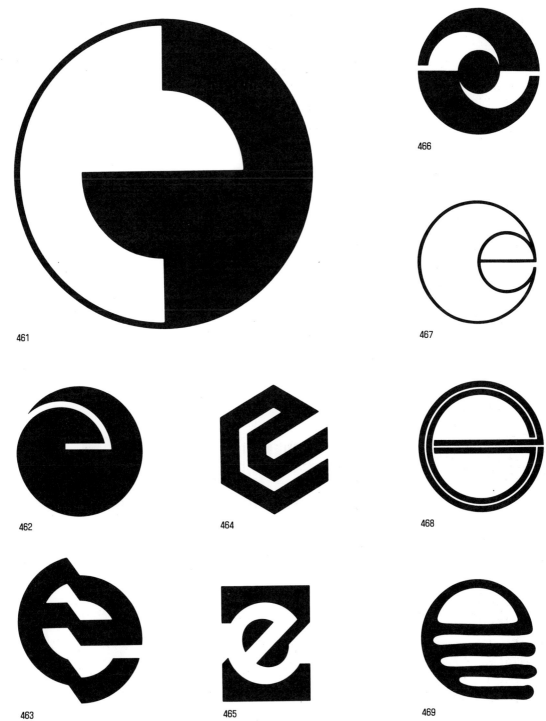

461

466

462

464

468

463

465

469

467

e

470

474

478

471

475

479

472

476

480

473

477

481

482

483

484

485

486

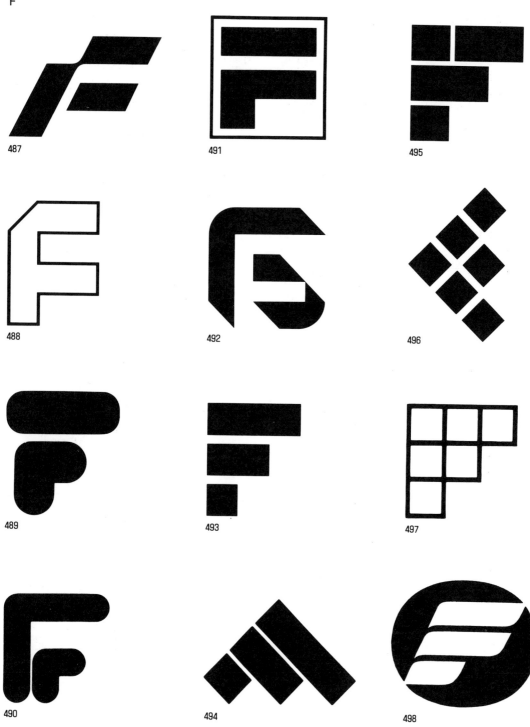

487

491

495

488

492

496

489

493

497

490

494

498

499

503

507

500

504

508

501

505

509

502

506

510

511

515

519

512

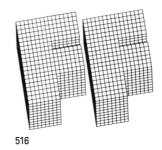

516

520

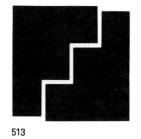

513

517

521

514

518

522

528

523

529

524

526

530

525

527

531

f

532

536

540

533

537

541

534

538

542

535

539

543

544

545

546

547

548

G

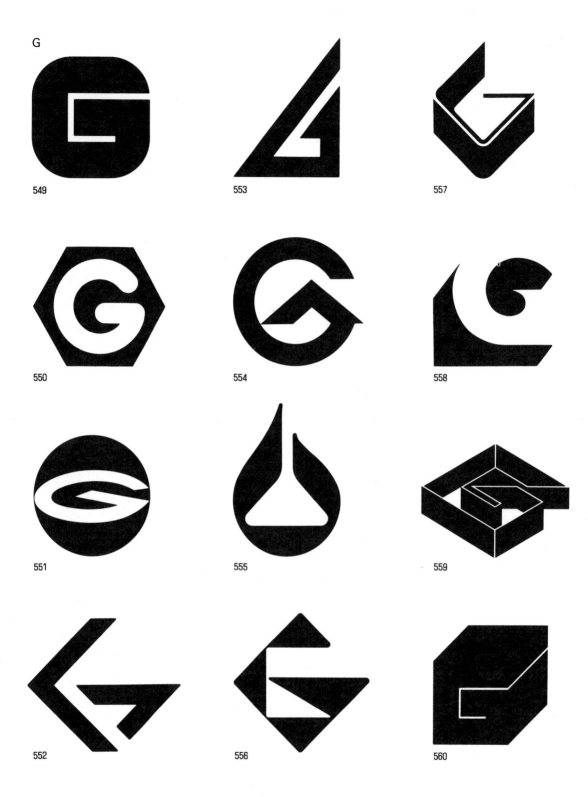

549

553

557

550

554

558

551

555

559

552

556

560

561

565

569

562

566

570

563

567

571

564

568

572

573

577

581

574

578

582

575

579

583

576

580

584

585

589

593

586

590

594

587

591

595

588

592

596

G

597

601

605

598

602

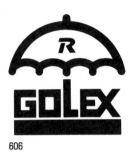

606

599

603

607

600

604

608

609

614

615

610

612

616

611

613

617

618

619

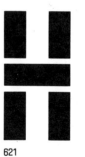

620

621

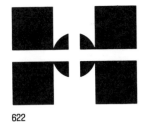

622

626

630

623

627

631

624

628

632

625

629

633

H

634

638

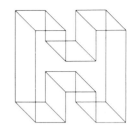

642

635

639

643

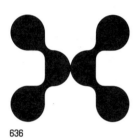

636

640

644

637

641

645

646

650

654

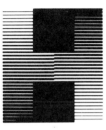

647

651

655

648

652

656

649

653

657

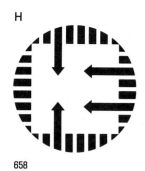

658

662

666

659

663

667

660

664

668

661

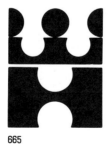

665

669

675

670

676

671

673

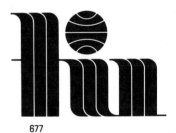

677

672

674

678

I

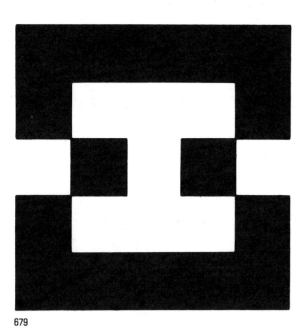

679

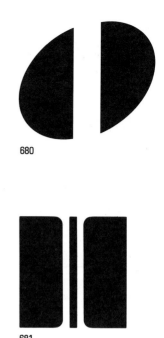

680

681

682

683

684

688

692

685

689

693

686

690

694

687

691

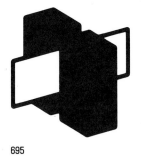

695

696

700

704

697

701

705

698

702

706

699

703

707

708

713

714

709

711

715

710

712

716

i

717

721

725

718

722

726

719

723

727

720

724

728

729

730

731

732

733

734

738

742

735

739

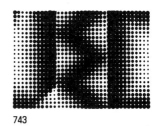

743

736

740

744

737

741

745

746

747

748

749

750

751

752

753

754

755

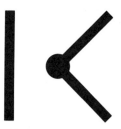

756

757

758

759

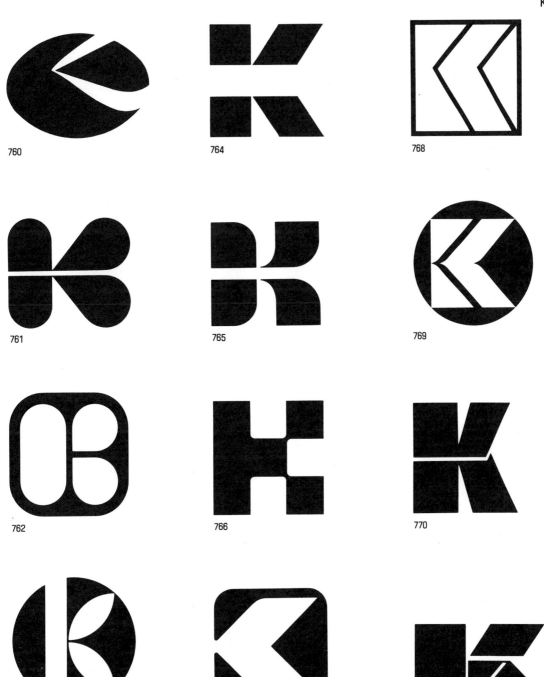

760

764

768

761

765

769

762

766

770

763

767

771

K

772

776

780

773

777

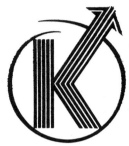

781

774

778

782

775

779

783

787

791

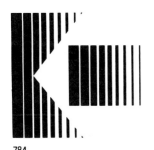

784

788

792

785

789

793

786

790

794

795

799

803

796

800

804

797

801

805

798

802

806

807

811

815

808

812

816

809

813

817

810

814

818

819

823

827

820

824

828

821

825

829

822

826

830

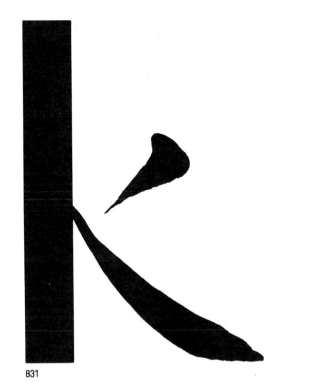

831

836

837

832

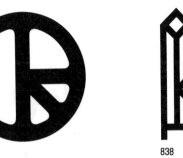

834

838

833

835

839

L

840

841

842

843

844

845

849

853

846

850

854

847

851

855

848

852

856

L

857

861

865

858

862

866

859

863

867

860

864

868

869

873

877

870

874

878

871

875

879

872

876

880

L

881

885

889

882

886

890

883

887

891

884

888

892

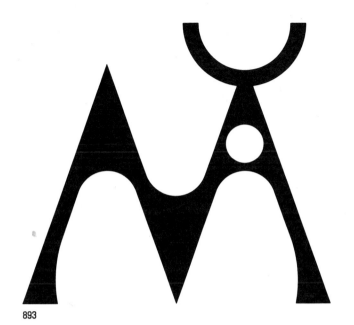

893

894

895

896

897

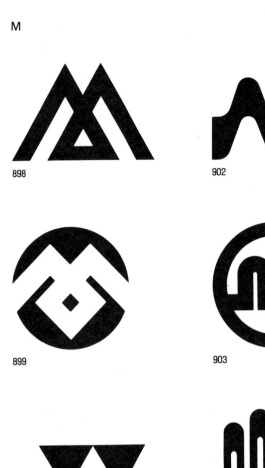

898

902

906

899

903

907

900

904

908

901

905

909

910

914

918

911

915

919

912

916

920

913

917

921

M

922

926

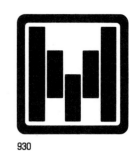
930

923

927

931

924

928

925

929

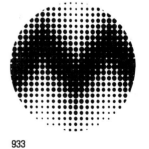
932

924

928

932

925

929

933

934

938

942

935

939

943

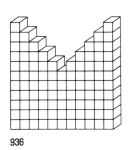

936

940

944

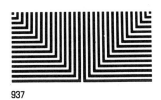

937

941

945

M

946

950

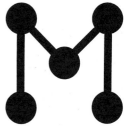

954

947

951

955

948

952

956

949

953

957

958

962

966

959

963

967

960

964

968

961

965

969

970

974

978

971

975

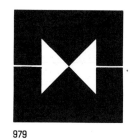

979

972

976

980

973

977

981

982

983

984

985

986

987

988

989

990

m

991

995

999

992

996

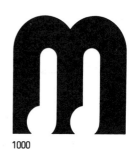

1000

993

997

1001

994

998

1002

1003

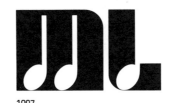

1007

1011

1004

1008

1012

1005

1009

1013

1006

1010

1014

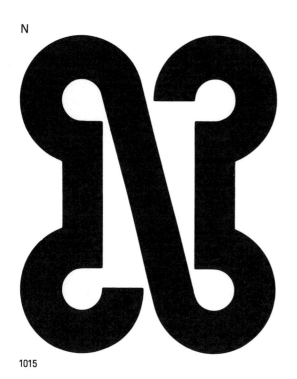

1015

1016

1017

1018

1019

1020

1024

1028

1021

1025

1029

1022

1026

1030

1023

1027

1031

1032

1036

1040

1033

1037

1041

1034

1038

1042

1035

1039

1043

1044

1048

1052

1045

1049

1053

1046

1050

1054

1047

1051

1055

1061

1056

1062

1057

1059

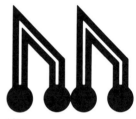

1063

1058

1060

1064

1065

1066

1067

1068

1069

O

1070

1074

1078

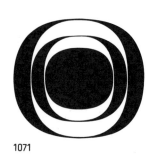

1071

1075

1079

1072

1076

1080

1073

1077

1081

1082

1086

1090

1083

1087

1091

1084

1088

1092

1085

1089

1093

1094

1095

1096

1097

1098

1099

1103

1107

1100

1104

1108

1101

1105

1109

1102

1106

1110

1111

1115

1119

1112

1116

1120

1113

1117

1121

1114

1118

1122

1123

1127

1131

1124

1128

1132

1125

1129

1133

1126

1130

1134

1135

1139

1143

1136

1140

1144

1137

1141

1145

1138

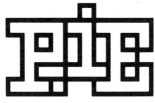

1142

1146

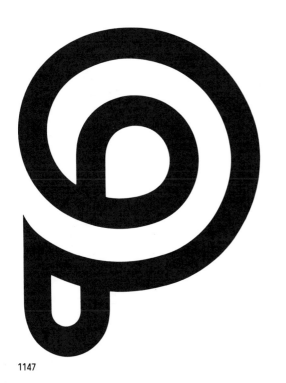

1147

1152

1153

1148

1150

1154

1149

1151

1155

p

1156

1160

1164

1157

1161

1165

1158

1162

1166

1159

1163

1167

1168

1172

1176

1169

1173

1177

1170

1174

1178

1171

1175

1179

1180

1181

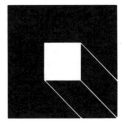

1182

1183

1184

1185

1189

1186

1190

1187

1191

1188

1192

1193

1194

1195

1196

1197

1198

1199

1200

1201

1202

1203

1204

1205

1206

1207

1208

1209

R

1210

1214

1218

1211

1215

1219

1212

1216

1220

1213

1217

1221

1222

1226

1230

1223

1227

1231

1224

1228

1232

1225

1229

1233

r

1234

1239

1240

1235

1237

1241

1236

1238

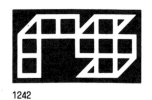

1242

1243

1244

1245

1246

1247

S

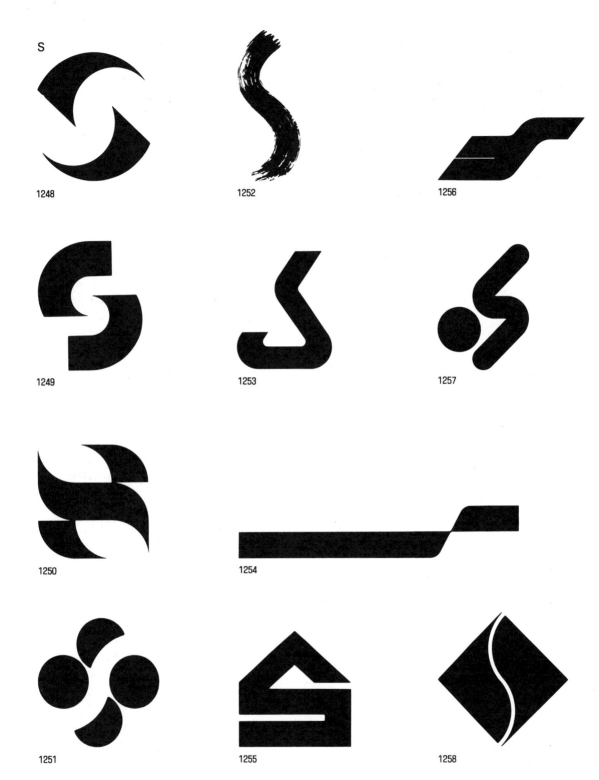

1248

1252

1256

1249

1253

1257

1250

1254

1251

1255

1258

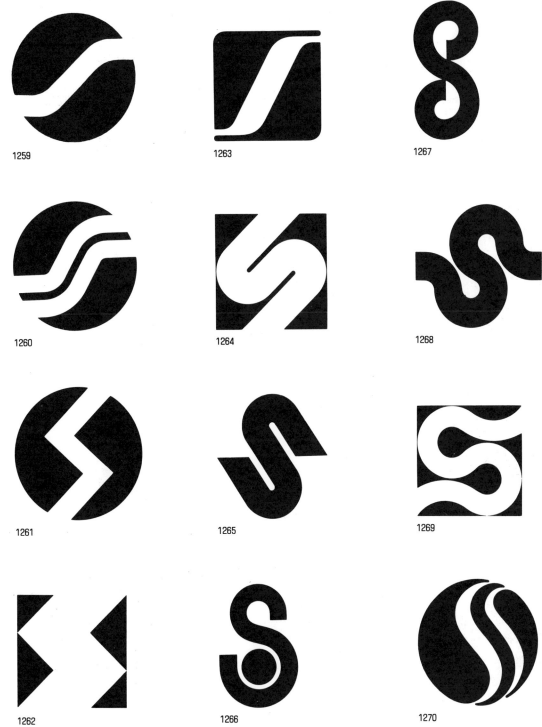

1259

1263

1267

1260

1264

1268

1261

1265

1269

1262

1266

1270

S

1271

1275

1279

1272

1276

1280

1273

1277

1281

1274

1278

1282

1283

1287

1291

1284

1288

1292

1285

1289

1293

1286

1290

1294

S

1295

1299

1303

1296

1300

1304

1297

1301

1305

1298

1302

1306

1307

1311

1315

1308

1312

1316

1309

1313

1317

1310

1314

1318

S

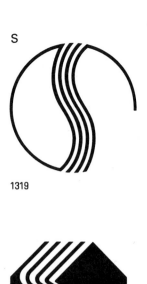

1319

1323

1327

1320

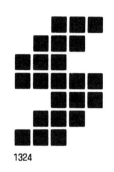

1324

1328

1321

1325

1329

1322

1326

1330

1331

1335

1339

1332

1336

1340

1333

1337

1341

1334

1338

1342

1343

1347

1351

1344

1348

1352

1345

1349

1353

1346

1350

1354

1355

1359

1363

1356

1360

1364

1357

1361

1365

1358

1362

1366

1367

1371

1375

1368

1372

1376

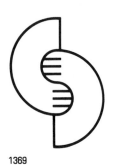

1369

1373

1377

1370

1374

1378

1379

1383

1387

1380

1384

1388

1381

1385

1389

1382

1386

1390

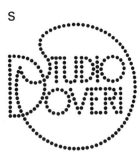

1391

1395

1399

1392

1396

1400

1393

1397

1401

1394

1398

1402

1404

1403

1405

1406

1407

T

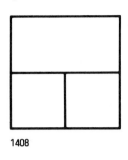

1408

1412

1416

1409

1413

1417

1410

1414

1418

1411

1415

1419

1420

1424

1428

1421

1425

1429

1422

1426

1430

1423

1427

1431

1432

1436

1440

1433

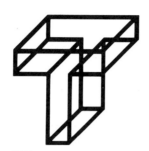

1437

1441

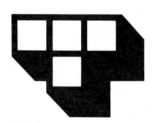

1434

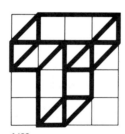

1438

1442

1435

1439

1443

1444

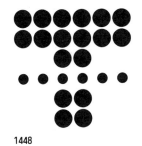

1448

1452

1445

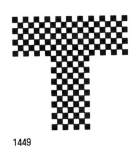

1449

1453

1446

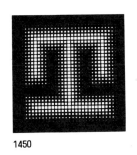

1450

1454

1447

1451

1455

T

1456

1460

1464

1457

1461

1465

1458

1462

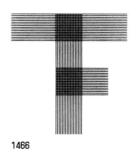

1466

1459

1463

1467

1468

1472

1476

1469

1473

1477

1470

1474

1478

1471

1475

1479

T

1480

1484

1488

1481

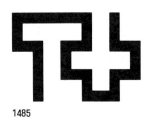

1485

1489

1482

1486

1490

1483

1487

1491

154

1492

1496

1500

1493

1497

1501

1494

1498

1502

1495

1499

1503

t

1504

1505

1506

1507

1508

1509

1510

1511

1512

1514

1513

1515

1516

1517

U

1518

1522

1526

1519

1523

1527

1520

1524

1528

1521

1525

1529

1530

1531

1534

1532

1535

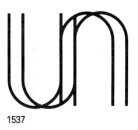

1537

1533

1536

1538

V

1539

1540

1541

1542

1543

1544

1548

1552

1545

1549

1553

1546

1550

1554

1547

1551

1555

V

1556

1560

1564

1557

1561

1565

1558

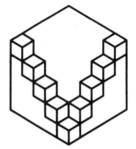

1562

1566

1559

1563

1567

1568

1576

1569

1573

1577

1570

1574

1578

1571

1575

1579

W

1580

1581

1582

1583

1584

1585

1589

1593

1586

1590

1594

1587

1591

1595

1588

1592

1596

1597

1601

1605

1598

1602

1606

1599

1603

1607

1600

1604

1608

1609

1613

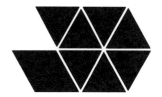

1617

1610

1614

1618

1611

1615

1619

1612

1616

1620

X

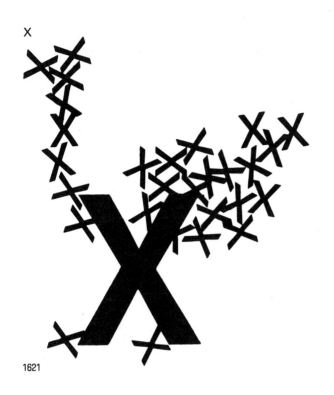

1621

1622

1623

1624

1625

1626

1630

1634

1627

1631

1635

1628

1632

1636

1629

1633

1637

1638

1639

1640

1641

1642

1643

1647

1651

1644

1648

1652

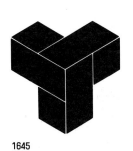

1645

1649

1653

1646

1650

1654

1655

1660

1661

1656

1658

1662

1657

1659

1663

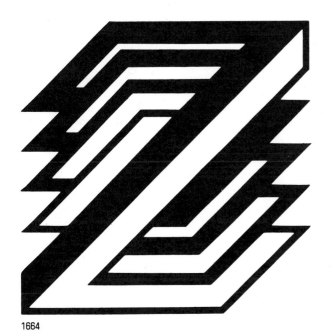

1664

1665

1666

1667

1668

Z

1669

1673

1677

1670

1674

1678

1671

1675

1672

1676

Index to contained works

1) Business Category
2) Art Director
3) Designer
4) Client
5) Year and Place Designed
6) Color

1 1) association of highways
3) Frutiger Adrian
4) Societe Francaise d' Autoroutes
5) 1975(France)
6) black
2 1) clothing
2),3) Kazumasa Nagai
4) Kashiyama Co., Ltd.
5) 1977(Japan)
6) green
3 1) finance(shinyo bank)
2),3) Kazumasa Nagai
4) Asahikawa Shinyo Bank
5) 1975(Japan)
4
2),3) Silvio Coppola
4) Area International
5) 1975(Milano)
5
2) Don Young
3) Don Young, Brian lovell, Anne Marie Morgante
4) The Douglas Allred Company
5) 1982(U.S.A.)
6 1) sport(tennis club)
2),3) Kazuo Tajima
4) Takaoka Royal Tennis Club
5) 1980(Japan)
6) light brown
7 1) type founding
2),3) Takahiro Shima
4) Artskana Co., Ltd.
5) 1982(Japan)
8 1) leasing
2),3) Silvio Coppola
4) Reggio Leasing
5) 1979(Milano)
9 1) architect
3) Guido Redaelli
4) architetto edo Zanaboni
5) 1978(Milano)
6) black
10 1) advertising agency
2),3) Oanh Pham-Phu
4) Anton Lihl
5) 1970(München)
6) orange
11 1) textile industry
2) Akira Hirata
3) Akira Hirata/Junko Naito
4) Vow Co., Ltd.
5) 1979(Japan)
6) dark gray(Pantone410C)
12 1) sporting goods
2),3) Kazumasa Nagai
4) Ben-General Corp.
5) 1980(Japan)
13 1) government of province
3) Paul Ibou
4) government of province of Antwerp

5) 1983(Belgium)
6) black(green/red)
14 1) educational institute
3) Akiteru Nakajima
4) Research Institute of Educational Facilities
5) 1973(Japan)
15 1) publishing
2),3) Yoshihiko Kurobe
4) Asunaro Academy
5) 1983(Japan)
16 1) antique
3) Carlo Malerba
4) Abrate Ferruccio
5) 1978(Italy)
17 1) electric machinery
2),3) Koichi Watanabe
4) Asahi parts Co., Ltd.
5) 1982(Japan)
18 1) housing apparatus
2),3) Akisato Ueda
4) Morioka Jutakukiki
5) 1975(Japan)
19 1) poster
2),3) Masakazu Tanabe
4) Aichiken Sangyo Design Kyogikai
5) 1977(Japan)
20 1) architect
2),3) Hiroshi Manzen
4) Asakura Architect & Associates
5) 1971(Japan)
21 1) computer
2),3) Minoru Takahashi
4) Academic Aye
5) 1980(Japan)
22 1) sport(club)
2),3) Shin Ikeda
4) Asari Sports Club Co.,Ltd.
5) 1980(Japan)
6) red(CF5036)
23 1) association(formative artists)
2),3) Fernando Medina
4) Artistas Plasticos Association
5) 1979(Madrid)
6) red
24 1) education(shodo kyoshitsu)
2),3) Hiroshi Toida
4) Asahi Shodo Kyoshitsu
5) 1980(Japan)
6) black
25 1) aerial photograph
2),3) Shinichi Takahara
4) Hokkaido Koku Shashin
5) 1980(Japan)
6) dark blue
26 1) energy
2),3) Ove Engström
4) Energy Storing System Inc. Co.
5) 1981(Sweden)
6) orange/red
27 1) association(construction technique)
3) Florent Garnier
4) private institute of construction technique
5) 1971(Lyon)
6) black/silver
28 1) metallurgical industry
2),3) João Carlos Cauduro/

Ludovico Antonio Martino
4) Nossa Senhora Aparecida
5) 1972(São Paulo)
29 1) school(college)
2),3) Hiroshi Toida
4) Akiyama Geijutsu Gakuin
5) 1982(Japan)
6) light reddish brown (VD0502)
30 1) architect
2),3) Dicken Castro
4) Annual of Architects Colombia
5) 1971(Colombia)
31 1) manufacturing(binding material)
2) Kazufumi Hamada
3) Akira Hirata/Hiroshi Mori
4) Alpha Techno Company
5) 1982(Japan)
32 1) trading
2) Kao Yu-Lin
3) Taipei Creative Center
4) AAA Trade & Investment Inc.
5) 1982(Taipei, Taiwan)
6) red/blue
33
2),3) Dicken Castro
4) Centro de Arte Actural
5) 1974(Colombia)
34 1) design studio
2) Yasunori Satake
3) Fumio Koyoda
4) Design Laboratory Adot
5) 1971(Japan)
35 1) resort
2),3) Jack Evans
4) Colorado Mountain Resort
5) (U.S.A.)
36 1) drive-in
2),3) Akisato Ueda
4) drive-in "Azuma"
5) 1975(Japan)
37
2),3) Kenichi Hirose
4) Sundelta Inc.
5) 1981(Japan)
6) blue
38 1) printing
3) Yoshikatsu Tami
4) Aoki Printing
5) 1979(Japan)
39 1) real estate
2),3) Shigeo Katsuoka
4) Asakura Co.
5) 1981(Japan)
6) blue purple(DIC222)
40 1) association(bottlers)
2),3) Ernesto Lehfeld
4) Anermex Bottlers Association
5) 1975(Mexico)
6) PMS144
41 1) road construction
2),3) Carl Christensen
4) ABC Asphalt
5) 1976(Oslo)
6) black
42 1) real estate
2) Duane Wiens
3) Carl Baden
4) Roxborough Park Development
5) 1979(U.S.A.)

6) rust
43
2) Dicken Castro
3) Dicken Castro/ Orlando Beltran/Nestor Munar
4) aerial fumigation for agriculture Alce
5) 1975(Colombia)
6) blue
44 1) airlines company
2),3) Felix Beltran
4) Ameriways/Miami
5) 1980(Mexico)
6) blue
45 1) hall
2),3) Armando Milani
4) Auditorium Midy Farmaceutici
5) 1974(Milano)
46 1) textile(wholesale)
2) Yukio Inamoto
3) Akisato Ueda
4) Sendan Co., Ltd.
5) 1974(Japan)
47 1) development
2),3) Akisato Ueda
4) Aoba Co., Ltd.
5) 1974(Japan)
48 1) cosmetic
2) Yakult Cosmetics(merchandise development section)
3) Yoshihiro Kishimoto
4) Yakult head office
5) 1977(Japan)
49 1) publishing(magazines)
2),3) Alfredo de Santis
4) Alitalia's Flight
5) 1971(Rome)
50 1) design studio
2),3) Eita Shinohara
4) Ace Design Office
5) 1975(Japan)
51 1) information(newspaper)
2),3) Shin Matsunaga
4) Nichigo Times
5) 1975(Japan)
52 1) association(livelihood cooperative)
2),3) PVDI
4) CCPL(central cooperative of dairy producers)
5) (Brazil)
53 1) motor accessories
2) Tomoko Taketomo
3) Hisako Ogura
4) Auto Craft Anzen
5) 1982(Japan)
54 1) private symbol(architect)
3) Rosmarie Tissi
4) Hans Bosshard
5) 1977(Zürich)
6) blue
55 1) duty free shop
2),3) Georg Staehelin
4) Empresa Nacional Aldeasa
5) 1977(Zürich)
6) red/yellow
56
2),3) Armando Milani
4) Antonio Hantegazza
5) 1975(Milano)
57 1) electric machinery
2) Armando Milani/ Maurizio Milani

Index to Contained Works

3) Maurizio Milani
4) Ambra Domestic Electric Appliances
5) 1979(Milano)
58
2),3) F.R.Esteban
4) McGraw Edison
5)1970(U.S.A.)
6) black
59 1) metallurgy
2),3) Jacques N.Garamond
4) "Arbed" metallurgical Industry
5) 1978(France)
6) black
60 1) tourism
2),3) Ivan Dvoršak
4) Alpeadria and Dos Ljubljana
5) 1981(Yugoslavia)
6) blue
61 1) publishing
2) Jolanta Baracz
3) Jarostaw Jasinski
4) Miodziezowa Publishing Agency
5) 1980(Warsaw)
6) black/many-coloured
62 1) association(arts)
2),3) Philip Gips
4) The American Federation of Arts
5) 1981(New York)
6) black
63 1) religion(church)
2),3) Gustavo Gomez -Casallas/
Rodrigo Fernandez
4) Catholic church
5) 1981(Colombia)
6) blue
64 1) design studio
2),3) Akiteru Nakajima
4) Art & Graphic
5) 1981(Japan)
65 1) association(artists)
2),3) Kazuo Kishimoto
4) Okinawa Artists Association
5) 1981(Japan)
66 1) interior(store)
2),3) Ikko Tanaka
4) Shop Heart Art
5) 1973(Japan)
67 1) association(mountaineers)
2),3) Miloš Ćirić
4) "Avala"
5) 1978(Beograd)
6) red
68 1) supermarket
2) Shakespear Design Studio
3) Raul Shakespear/
Ronald Shakespear
4) Acasso Supermarket
5) 1982(Buenos Aires)
6) red/green
69 1) cemetery
2),3) Santos Paniagua
4) Milwaukee Memorial Co.
5) 1976(Milwaukee)
6) green/dark gray
70 1) fishing
2),3) Guillermo Gonzalez Ruiz
4) "Anchomar" Fishing

Company
5) 1979(Buenos Aires)
6) sky blue
71 1) aerial photograph
2),3) Allan W.Miller
4) Aerotopo
5) 1981(U.S.A.)
6) brown/black
72 1) hotel
2),3) Stephan Kantscheff
4) Astoria
5) 1976(Bulgaria)
73 1) cosmetic
2),3) Stephan Kantscheff
4) Aloma
5) 1977(Bulgaria)
74 1) publishing
2),3) Marty Neumeier
4) Avant Cards
5) 1977(U.S.A.)
6) black
75 1) research
2),3) James Lienhart
4) Allan Cox & Associates
5) (Chicago)
76 1) accountant
3) Paul Ibou
4) Accountantskantoor A.D.
5) 1970(Belgium)
77 1) music(group)
3) Nikola Nikolov
4) "Dobrudja"
5) 1983(Bulgaria)
6) black/white
78 1) energy(oil,gas)
2),3) Jack Evans
4) American Empire Oil & Gas, Inc.
5) (U.S.A.)
79 1) foundation
2),3) Don Connelly
4) Arthritis Foundation
5) 1977(U.S.A.)
6) blue
80 1) bicycle accessory (manufacture)
2),3) Fumio Koyoda
4) Aotani Kogyo
5) 1981(Japan)
81 1) private symbol (musician)
2) Calvin Woo
3) Calvin Woo/Eric Woo
4) Arthur Joseph
5) 1980(U.S.A.)
6) light blue/burgundy
82 1) airport
2),3) Ivan Dvorsak
4) Maribor airport
5) 1976(Yugoslavia)
6) blue
83 1) motion picture producer
2),3) Edward Hughes
4) Arc Light Productions
5) 1979(U.S.A.)
6) black
84 1) research institute (medicine)
2) Micheal Richards
3) Bill Swensen
4) University of Utah Medical Center
5) 1980(U.S.A.)
6) red

85
2),3) Pietro Galli
4) Antonelli Vivai-Pavia
5) 1976(Italy)
6) green
86 1) advertising agency
2),3) Tadamasa Katsube
4) Ai-Planning
5) 1983(Japan)
87 1) airport (business)
2),3) Frutiger Adrian
4) Airport of Paris
5) 1971(France)
6) black
88 1) manufacturing(frames)
2),3) Walter Hergenröther
4) Aspa-Plast-System
5) 1977(Italy)
6) red/black
89 1) motor dealer
2),3) Shin Matsunaga/
Osamu Furuta
4) Autorama
5) 1982(Japan)
6) Manser7.5RP4.4/15.4
90 1) museum
2),3) Nikola Nikolov
4) Art Gallery the Town of Sliven
5) 1979(Bulgaria)
6) black
91 1) industry
2),3) Selahattin Sönmez
4) Azote Industry
5) 1973(Istanbul)
6) blue
92
2),3) Arthur Eckstein
4) American Scale Corp.
5) 1980(New York)
6) blue(PMS285)
93 1) interior(shop)
2),3) Gerd Leufert
4) Sistemas Ambientales
5) 1981(Venezuela)
6) black
94 1) private symbol (designer)
2),3) Ernesto Lehfeld
4) Aros-Throndson, S.C.
5) 1980(Mexico)
6) PMS170
95 1) electric machinery
2),3) Jack Evans
4) Adaptive Test
5) 1983(U.S.A.)
6) blue/silver
96 1) stockbroker
2),3) Fernando Rión
4) Acciones y Valores
5) 1979(Mexico)
6) blue
97
3) Paul Ibou
4) Akademisch Ziekenhuis Antwerpen
5) 1978(Belgium)
98 1) electric machinery
2),3) Walter Hergenrother
4) ACFIS
5) 1973(Italy)
6) blue/turquoise
99 1) back-up services for oil industry
2),3) Tor Pettersen

4) Alireza Group, Kuwait
5) 1970(London)
6) black
100 1) publishing
3) Frutiger Adrian
5) 1976(France)
6) black
101 1) commerical film
2),3) Robert Hargenhoffer
4) Auleama International Group
5) (U.S.A.)
102
2),3) Roger Remington
4) Artpark, Inc.
5) 1978(New York)
6) PMS reflex blue
103 1) rubber manufacturing
2),3) Don Connelly
4) Associated Rubber Co.
5) 1981(U.S.A.)
6) red
104 1) association (university administration)
2),3) Don Nichols
4) American Association of University Administration
5) 1970(New York)
6) blue
105 1) broadcasting
2),3) Philip Gips
4) American Broadcasting Co.
5) 1976(New York)
6) blue/red
106 1) computer communications Co.
2),3) Conrad E.Angone
4) American Computer and Communications Company
5) 1971(Los Angeles)
6) dark blue
107 1) fiberglass industry
2),3) Terry Lesniewicz/
Al Navarre
4) Owens-Corning Fiberglass Corporation
5) 1983(U.S.A.)
108 1) store
2) Joe Selame
3) Selame Design Group
4) TG&Y Stores
5) 1982(U.S.A.)
6) terracotta
109 1) stationary
2),3) Stephan Kantscheff
4) Allen Mac
5) 1971(Bulgaria)
110 1) development
2) Jack Weiss
3) Randi Robin
4) American Planning Associantion
5) 1979(U.S.A.)
6) blue
111 1) computer
2),3) Bruce D.Zahor
4) Apro System Co.
5) 1982(New York)
112 1) sport(association)
2) Shiro Koseki
3) Katsuhiko Maki
4) Aerospace Scouts Association
5) 1983(Japan)
6) red/dark blue

13
),3) Peter G.Ulmer
AVL AG.Schaffhausen
) 1975(Switzerland)
) blue
14
),3) Fernando Medina
Arte
) 1982(Madrid)
) red
15 1) school(design)
A.G.Fronzoni
) Studio di Architettura
) 1981(Milano)
) black
16 1) insurance company
),3) Manfred Korten
Lüttgen Insurance Company
) 1981(West Germany)
) black
17 1) automatic operation
),3) Madeleine Bujatti
) Fröhlich
) 1976(Austria)
) blue/red/black
18 1) printing
),3) Burton Kramer
) Aerographics Lithographers
) 1975(Toronto)
) red/blue/yellow
119 1) design studio
2),3) Kazuo Oono
4) Studio Eye
5) 1978(Japan)
120 1) automotive industry
2),3) Marty Neumeier
4) Arntz Cobra
5) 1980(U.S.A.)
6) black
121 1) autosalon
2),3) Michael Heroed
4) Stuttgarter Messe und
Kongress GmbH
5) 1983(West Germany)
6) blue/pink
122
2),3) Don Davis
4) Alpha Group
5) 1974(U.S.A.)
6) black
123
2),3) Peter Wildbur
4) Visiting Arts Unit
5) 1982(London)
124 1) planning and
construction of shop and
interior
2),3) Othmar Motter
4) Josef Armellini KG
5) 1973(Austria)
6) black/white
125 1) civil institution
of development
2),3) Rey Da Costa R.
4) Civil Association of
Development Institution
5) 1978(Venezuela)
6) dark brown
126 1) paper-manufacturing
2),3) Burton Kramer
4) Anglo-Canadian Paper Co.
5) 1973(Toronto)
6) green
127
2) Gunter Mohr

3) Gary Ball
4) Agripac Inc.
5) 1972(U.S.A.)
6) green
128 1) private symbol
2),3) Don Davis
4) Don Davis
5) 1971(U.S.A.)
6) black
129 1) oil stove
manufacturing
3) Szekeres István
4) Mechanikai Müvek
5) 1970(Budapest)
6) black
130 1) manufacturing
2),3) Don Davis
4) Armbruster Mfg.
5) 1975(U.S.A.)
6) gray/red
131 1) food
(manufacturing and selling)
2),3) Saul Bass
4) Ajinomoto
5) 1973(Los Angeles)
132 1) hotel
2),3) Stephan Kantscheff
4) Ambassador
5) 1976(Bulgaria)
133 1) advertising agency
2),3) Jack Evans
4) Allday & Associates
5) (U.S.A.)
134 1) construction
2),3) Stephan Kantscheff
4) Albena
5) 1971(Bulgaria)
6) red/purple/yellow
135 1) hotel
2),3) Stephan Kantscheff
4) Acacia
5) 1976(Bulgaria)
136 1) shopping center
2) Keith Murgatroyd
3) Tony Forster
4) Newton Ards Shopping
Centre
5) 1974/1978(London)
6) red/blue
137 1) design studio
3) Fred E.Denzler
4) Aephus Designs
5) 1973(U.S.A.)
6) black
138 1) printing
(lithographer)
3) Fred E.Denzler
4) Argus Press
5) 1976(U.S.A.)
6) multi-colored
139 1) lighting
(manufacturing)
2),3) Ray Engle
4) Architectural Area
Lighting Co.
5) 1970(Los Angeles)
6) many
140 1) sports club
2),3) Don Connelly
4) Avondale Swim & Tennis
club
5) 1979(U.S.A.)
6) green
141 1) soil testing
2),3) Ed Penniman

4) Ames Soil Testing
5) 1980(U.S.A.)
6) PMS522/398
142 1) savings bank
2),3) Elias Garcia Benavides
4) Asturlas Savings Bank
5) 1983(Spain)
6) blue
143 1) radio/television
research
2),3) Jack Evans
4) Audience Development Inc.
5) (U.S.A.)
144 1) atelier
3) Michael Herold
4) Relindis Agethen
5) 1974(West Germany)
6) black
145 1) bank
3) Peter Skalar
4) Adria Bank
5) 1980(Yugoslavia)
6) blue
146 1) product distrbution
2),3) Molfos Diseño S.C.
4) A.C.Distribuidora, S.A.
5) 1983(Mexico)
6) warm gray
147 1) furniture
manufacturer
2),3) Rinaldo Cutini
4) Castagna Arredamenti
5) 1973(Rome)
6) black
148
3) Frutiger Adrian
4) Institut Atlantique Paris
5) 1980(France)
6) black
149
2),3) Don Connelly
4) Automated Marketing
5) 1983(U.S.A.)
6) blue
150 1) packaging
2),3) William Carson
4) Advance Packaging Inc.
5) 1975(U.S.A.)
6) orange/brown
151 1) printing
2),3) Robert Hargenhoffer
4) Ansbacker Siegel Printing
Co.
5) (U.S.A.)
152 1) automotive industry
2),3) Kiyoshi Kyoi
4) Honda Giken Kogyo Co.
5) 1977(Japan)
6) Toyo CF5062
153 1) letter manufacturer
2),3) Richard Wittosch
4) Alphabet Shop Inc.
5) 1971(U.S.A.)
6) red/blue
154 1) tourism
2),3) Armin Vogt
4) Airtour Suisse S.A.
5) 1981(Switzerland)
6) Pantone warm red
155 1) interior
2),3) Othmar Motter
4) Studio AX
5) 1979(Austria)
6) black/white
156 1) association(graphic art)

2),3) José Santamarina
4) Association of Managers
of Graphic Art
5) 1973(Spain)
6) blue/yellow/black
157 1) factory
3) Velizar Petrov
4) Factory "Boriana"
5) 1982(Bulgaria)
158 1) alcohol information and
counseling
2) Thomas Ohmer
3) Carl Seltzer
4) Alcoholism Information
Center
5) 1976(Los Angeles)
6) red
159 1) night club
2),3) Othmar Motter
4) Night-Club "Bodensee"
5) 1974(Austria)
6) black/white
160 1) textile industry
2) Akira Hirata
3) Akira Hirata/Yoshiharu
Saito
4) Bellfeed Co., Ltd.
5) 1980(Japan)
6) Pantone287c
161 1) machine industry
3) Guido Redaelli
4) Bertuzzi S.A.
5) 1970(Milano)
6) black
162 1) publishing
2),3) Makoto Yoshida
4) Bunka Hyoronsha
5) 1982(Japan)
6) brown(CF5057)/black
163 1) cosmetic
2),3) Fumio Koyoda
4) Max Co., Ltd.
5) 1981(Japan)
164 1) interior
2) Soyster & Ohrenschall, Inc.
3) Ed Penniman
4) Breuners Furniture Co.
5) 1971(U.S.A.)
6) PMS469
165 1) "all for the baby" shop
2),3) Othmar Motter
4) "Alles für das Baby"
5) 1982(Austria)
6) black/white
166 1) printing
2),3) Jack Evans
4) Bennetts
5) (U.S.A.)
167 1) publishing
2),3) Yasaburo Kuwayama
4) Big Company
5) 1980(Japan)
168
3) Paul Ibou
4) Biblo
5) 1981(Belgium)
169 1) architect
2),3) Gale William Ikola
4) R.W.Buelow Architects
5) 1981(U.S.A.)
6) brown
170 1) construction
2),3) Peter G.Ulmar
4) Bolli Bauunternehmung
5) 1977(Switzerland)

6) orange
171 1) private symbol(hatmaker)
2),3) Oanh Pham-Phu
4) Breiter Hatmaker
5) 1970(München)
6) gray
172 1) construction
2) Ronald Cutro
3) Cutro Associates, Inc.
4) Custom Builders, Inc.
5) 1980(U.S.A.)
6) black
173 1) real estate
2),3) Terry Lesniewicz/ Al Navarre
4) Bailey Real Estate
5) 1979(U.S.A.)
174 1) gas and waterwork
2),3) Othmar Motter
4) gas and waterworks, Bregenz
5) 1980(Austria)
6) black/white
175
3) Frutiger Adrian
4) Energies Nouvelles "Novelerg"
5) 1978(France)
6) black
176 1) design studio
2),3) Linda N. Reuter
4) Bountiful Art Center
5) 1974(U.S.A.)
6) purple
177 1) book store
2) Michael Richards
3) Michael Mabry
4) Bjok Store-University of Utah
5) 1978(U.S.A.)
178 1) manufacturing(razor blades)
2),3) Carlos Rolando
4) Luis Bassat
5) 1972(Venezuela)
6) black/silver
179
2),3) Armin Vogt
4) Belair AG
5) 1979(Switzerland)
6) Pantone warm red
180 1) porcelain
2),3) Rockford Mjos
4) Bryant Porcelain
5) 1983(U.S.A.)
6) Pantone194
181 1) symphony orchestra
2),3) Othmar Motter
4) Bodensee Symphonie -Orchestra
5) 1983(Austria)
6) black/white
182 1) interior
2),3) Stephan Kantscheff
4) Bida
5) 1981(Bulgaria)
183 1) Hotel and joint control
2),3) Molfos Diseño S.C.
4) Real Estate Promotion of Sureste S.A.
5) 1980(Mexico)
6) blue
184 1) sport(golf club)
2),3) Ernesto Lehfeld

4) Bellavista Golf Club
5) 1971(Mexico)
6) PMS364
185
2),3) Terry Lesniewicz/Al Navarre
4) Bostleman Corporation
5) 1973(U.S.A.)
186
2),3) Burton Kramer
4) Bell Canada
5) 1976(Toronto)
6) blue
187
2) Gottschalk+Ash International
3) Stuart Ash
4) Ber Gold Inc.
5) 1976(Toronto)
188 1) textile(marketing)
2) Sudarshan Dheer
3) Ashok Sood
4) Bombay Market
5) 1976(Bombay)
6) green/blue
189 1) banking
2),3) Jorge Canales
4) National Bank of Fishing Port
5) 1981(Mexico)
6) blue/green
190 1) church
2),3) Gale William Ikola
4) Brunswick United Methodist Church
5) 1971(U.S.A.)
6) blue
191 1) publishing
3) Szekeres Ístván
4) Buvár/Diver/Zsebkönyvek
5) 1971(Budapest)
6) black
192 1) drink(manufacturing)
3) G.Edwards
4) Balseca
5) 1978(Mexico)
6) blue
193 1) chemical for agriculture (manufacturing)
2),3) Leen Averink
4) Bayer-France
5) 1978(France)
194 1) design studio
2),3) Armando Milani
4) Tre B Design
5) 1975(Milano)
195
2),3) Tim Larsen
4) Bather, Belrose, Boje Inc.
5) 1981(U.S.A.)
6) black
196 1) consultant
2),3) Burton Kramer
4) Bedford consulting Group
5) 1981(Toronto)
6) gold
19 1) bank
2) Yvett & Roland Michau
3) Rudi Meyer
4) Banque Nationale de Paris
5) 1974(France)
6) black/white
198 1) hotel
2) John Follis

3) T.Wayne Hunt
4) The Biltmore Hotel
5) 1976(Los Angeles)
199 1) art gallery
2),3) Angelo Sganzerla
4) Borgogna art gallery
5) 1970(Milano)
6) black
200 1) bakery
3) Rosmarie Tissi
4) Backerei Burkhard
5) 1973(Switzerland)
6) brown
201 1) chemical (wholesale trade)
3) A.G.Schillemans
4) Brunschwig Chemie
5) 1979(Amsterdam)
6) blue
202
2),3) Stephan Kantscheff
4) Bitwa Estetica
5) 1972(Bulgaria)
203 1) interior
2),3) Stephan Kantscheff
4) Bitosia
5) 1981(Bulgaria)
204 1) fence(manufacturing)
2) Ben Bos
3) Ben Bos/Evert Snellenberg
4) B&G Hekwerken
5) 1978(Amsterdam)
6) orange(Pantone orange OZIU)
205 1) bank
2),3) Chermayeff & Geismar Associates
4) Banco de Italia y Rio de la Plata
5) (U.S.A.)
6) green
206
3) Paul Ibou
4) Belgische Lloyd
5) 1971(Belgium)
207 1) bankers contest
2),3) Francesco Burcini
4) Banco Larino
5) 1979(Italy)
6) green
208 1) book store
2) Osamu Ogawa
3) Junzo Yamamoto
4) Miyamaru
5) 1978(Japan)
209 1) bank
3) Miani Luigi/Guido Redaelli
4) Banka Rasini
5) 1973(Milano)
210 1) paper industry
2) Takeshi Nakajima
3) Takeo Sugaya
4) Boso Shigyo Co., Ltd.
5) 1977(Japan)
211 1) finance
2),3) Tony Forster
4) Bridgeway Finance, Ltd.
5) 1976(London)
6) gold
212 1) architecture and exhibition company
2),3) Giovanni Brunazzi
4) Groupo Bodino
5) 1979(Italy)
213 1) cosmetic(selling)

2),3) Yoriya Ueda
4) Kanebo Cosmetics
5) 1974(Japan)
214 1) architect
2),3) Frances Ullenberg
4) BHS Architecture
5) 1980(U.S.A.)
6) dark gray
215 1) group of industry
2),3) Sudarshan Dheer
4) Ballarpur Industries, Ltd.
5) 1975(Bombay)
6) olive green/black
216 1) interior(furniture)
2) Shigeo Katsuoka
3) Shigeo Katsuoka/Hiroshi Asami
4) Maruichi Saling
5) 1982(Japan)
217 1) private symbol(engineer)
2),3) Manfred Wutke
4) B.Mohamed Badawi
5) 1980(Egypt)
6) black
218 1) association(bookcraft)
2),3) Adam Moltke
4) The Society of Bookcraft
5) 1982(Denmark)
6) black
219 1) chain of optician
3) A.G.Schillemans
4) Brilmij Glasses Store
5) 1975(Netherlands)
6) light blue
220 1) fiberglas (manufacturing)
2),3) Terry Lesniewics/Al Navarre
4) Owens-Corning Fiberglas Coroporation
5) 1983(U.S.A.)
221 1) underwear (manufacturing)
2),3) Robert P.Gersin
4) BVD-Union Underwear
5) 1978(New York)
6) white
222 1) building material trading
2),3) Walter Hergenröther
4) Bauwaren Bozen
5) 1979(Italy)
6) green/dark blue
223 1) bank
2),3) Peter G.Ulmer
4) Bankinstitute Zurich
5) 1982(Zurich)
6) gold
224 1) bank
2),3) Othmar Motter
4) Bank for Tirol and Vorarlberg
5) 1982(Austria)
6) black/white
225
2) Anton Stankowski/Duschek
3) Anton Stankowski
4) Stadt Brühl
5) 1971(West Germany)
226 1) bank
2),3) George Tscherny
4) R.L.Banks & Associates
5) 1972(New York)
6) black

227 1) textile industry
3) Matjaž Bertonceli
4) BPT
5) 1975(Yugoslavia)
6) blue
228 1) furniture
(manufacturing)
2),3) Shunji Ninomi
4) Houtoku Furniture
5) 1980(Japan)
229 1) heater(manufacturing)
2),3) Francesco Burcini
4) Bartolini
5) 1977(Italy)
6) brown
230 1) festival
2),3) Othmar Motter
4) Festival of Bregenz
5) 1983(Austria)
6) black/white
231 1) hosiery
2),3) Francesco Burcini
4) Batori
5) 1982(Italy)
6) brown/orange
232 1) private symbol
2),3) James Lienhart
4) Becky Bisioulis
5) (Chicago)
233 1) bank
2),3) Jack Evans
4) Bank of Dallas
5) 1982(U.S.A.)
6) dark purple/gray
234 1) boutique(underwear for
women)
2),3) Yasumasa Oka
4) Belair
5) 1979(Japan)
235
2),3) Rockford Mjos
4) Blaine Karsten & Deirdre
Michael
5) 1976(U.S.A.)
6) gold
236 1) private symbol(Farber)
2),3) Helmut Salden
4) Barbara Farber
5) 1971(Amsterdam)
237 1) pharmaceutical
laboratory
2),3) F.R.Esteban
4) Bio Decision Laboratories
5) 1971(U.S.A.)
6) black
238 1) funeral service
2) Margaret S.Brown
3) John S.Brown
4) Bay of Quinte Funeral
Service Association
5) 1981(Canada)
6) gold
239 1) food industry
2),3) Hiroyuki Okuda
4) Bunnosuke Syokuhin
5) 1978(Japan)
240 1) series of international
finance lecture
2),3) Edward Hughes
4) Roosevelt University
5) 1971(U.S.A.)
241 1) paper industry
3) Kenneth Hollick
4) British Tissues Ltd.
5) 1976(London)

6) red/blue/white
242 1) architect
2) Robert L.Willis
3) Vicky Ko
4) Browning,Day,Pollak
Associates
5) 1975(U.S.A.)
6) black
243 1) real estate
2),3) Azar Khosrovi-Ivorsohk
4) Stephan Zucker &
Associates
5) 1981(New York)
6) turquoise(Pantone343)
244
2),3) Kenneth Hollick
4) Blackall Cooke and Dew,
Ltd.
5) 1983(London)
6) red
245 1) art gallery
2),3) Gerd Leufert
4) Galería Conkright
5) 1973(Venezuela)
6) black
246 1) manufacturing
2),3) Stephan Kantscheff
4) Septembri
5) 1979(Bulgaria)
247 1) glaswork
2) Vincenc Kutač
3) Stanislav Kovář
4) Crystalex Nový Bor
5) 1973(Czechoslovakia)
6) light blue
248 1) photographic design
studio
2) Ted Cartwright
3) Tony Forster
4) Cartwright Studios, Ltd.
5) 1979(Manchester)
6) black
249 1) conference
2) Ikko Tanaka
3) Ikko Tanaka/Tetsuya Oota
4) World Craft Conferance
5) 1978(Japan)
250 1) food processing
2),3) Yukio Kanise
4) Chiyoda Karashi Honpo
5) 1971(Japan)
251 1) exhibition house of
ocean culture
2),3) Ikko Tanaka
4) JETRO
5) 1974(Japan)
252 1) industrial park
3) Robert A.Gale
4) Ram Ridge Corporate Park
5) 1975(New York)
6) black
253 1) printing
2),3) Marty Neumeier
4) Chroma Litho
5) 1983(U.S.A.)
6) black
254 1) bank
2),3) Richard Yeager
4) Commerce Bank
5) 1973(U.S.A.)
6) black/red
255 1) design studio
2) Ove Engström
3) Ingvar Johansson
4) Ove Engström AB

5) 1983(Sweden)
6) gray
256 1) industry
2),3) Stephan Kantscheff
4) Septembri
5) 1972(Bulgaria)
257 1) optical instrument(neon
industries)
2) Gottschalk+Ash
International
3) Stuart Ash/Fredy Jaggie/
Fritz Gottschalk
4) Claude Neon Industries Ltd.
5) 1973(Toronto)
258 1) printing
2),3) James Lienhart
4) Chicago Graphics, Inc.
5) (Chicago)
259 1) cement product
2),3) Bill Bundzak
4) Coplay Cement Co.
5) 1979(New York)
6) blue
260 1) chemical industry
2) Maurizio Milani/Armando
Milani
3) Maurizio Milani
4) Chimica del Friuli
5) 1981(Milano)
261
3) Hugo Arape
4) Cayena
5) 1978(France)
6) red
262 1) bag maker
2),3) Dicken Castro
4) Colombian Bags
5) 1978(Colombia)
263 1) technology
2),3) Roger Remington
4) Clark Technologies
5) 1975(New York)
6) red(Pantone485u)
264 1) medicine
(manufacturing)
2),3) Ernst Roch
4) Pharmacie Centre
5) 1975(Montreal)
265 1) grain handling
2) Takenobu Igarashi
3) Takenobu Igarashi/Hiroshi
Asami
4) Chiba Grain Handling
Center,Ltd.
5) 1981(Japan)
266 1) computer
2),3) Yuji Baba
4) Nippon Computer Co.
5) 1971(Japan)
267 1) transportation
2),3) José Santamarina
4) Carcaba
5) 1982(Spain)
6) red
268
2),3) Guillermo Gonzalez Ruiz
4) Credit Card
5) 1978(Buenos Aires)
6) blue/green
269 1) design and public
relation
2),3) Rinaldo Cutini
4) Bonaria Casu
5) 1974(Rome)
6) red

270 1) packing material maker
2),3) Koichi Watanabe
4) Canpack Corp.
5) 1975(Japan)
271 1) fitting up lithofilm
3) Walter Hergenröter
4) Offset Montage Center
5) 1977(Italy)
6) red/brown
272
2),3) PVDI
4) Grupo Crefisul
5) 1976(Brazil)
273
2),3) Dicken Castro
4) Central Meeting of Conzalo
Jimenez de Quesada
5) 1979(Colombia)
274 1) industry
2),3) Alfredo de Santis
4) Casagrande Impianti
5) 1983(Rome)
275 1) office
machine(manufacturing)
2),3) Minoru Takahashi
4) Canon
5) 1983(Japan)
276 1) education
2),3) Sadao Sugaya
4) Kokusai Communications
5) 1979(Japan)
6) blue
277 1) bank
2),3) Silvio Gayton
4) Central National Bank
5) 1980(U.S.A.)
6) gray/black
278 1) culture market
2),3) Dieter Urban
4) Kulturmarkt Dillingen
5) 1980(Brussels)
279 1) metallurgy
2),3) Florent Garnier
4) Cefilac
5) 1971(Lyon)
6) black
280
2),3) Ettore Vitale
4) Comforto
5) 1974(Rome)
281
2),3) Dicken Castro
4) Compartir
5) 1980(Colombia)
282 1) association(architects)
2) Burton Kramer
3) Karl Märtens/Burton
Kramer
4) Ontario Association of
Architects
5) 1980(Toronto)
6) red/orange
283 1) travel agency
2),3) D.Bruce Zahor
4) Command Travel, Inc.
5) 1978(New York)
6) blue/white
284 1) trade(exporter)
2),3) Felix Beltran
4) Cimeo Milan
5) 1980(Mexico)
6) brown
285 1) interior maintenance
and renovation service
2) Thomas Ohmer

3) Koji Takei
4) Commercial Industrial Systems
5) 1981(Los Angeles)
6) yellow／ochre／black
286
2),3) Michael Vanderbyl
4) The Court
5) 1978(San Francisco)
6) black
287 1) hotel
3) A.G.Fronzoni
4) Le Canne Hotel
5) 1972(Milano)
6) black
288 1) broadcasting
2),3) Burton Kramer
4) Canadian Broadcasting Corporation
5) 1974(Toronto)
6) red／orange red／orange／yellow
289
2),3) Burton Kramer
4) Centre Stage Company
5) 1982(Toronto)
6) red
290
2),3) Los Shakespear
5) (Buenos Aires)
291
2),3) Gustavo Gomez -Casallas／Rodrigo Fernandez
4) Colombia Natural
5) 1978(Colombia)
6) sienna
292 1) insurance
2),3) Gustavo Gomez -Casallas／Rodrigo Fernandes
4) CONASE
5) 1976(Colombia)
6) blue／gray
293 1) interior
2),3) Stephan Kantscheff
4) Rebed
5) 1970(Bulgaria)
294 1) finance
2),3) Denise Spaulding
4) Cardinal Federal
5) 1980(U.S.A.)
6) red／gray
295 1) travel agency
2),3) U.G.Sato
4) Canadian Coco Tours
5) 1982(Japan)
6) blue
296 1) hotel
2),3) Fernando Rion
4) Hoteles Continental
5) 1978(Mexico)
6) orange／brown／red
297 1) paint for ship
2),3) Tsuneo Arima
4) Ihara Chemical Co.,Ltd.
5) 1983(Japan)
6) green／purple
298 1) association(cooks)
2),3) Julien Van Der Wal
4) Cuisine de L'Amitie
5) 1977(Geneve)
6) black／red
299 1) trade
2),3) Maurizio Milani
4) Cotrako
5) 1982(Milano)

300 1) committee
3) Nikola Nikolov
4) Committee for Burgarian Soviet Friendship
5) 1983(Bulgaria)
6) black／white
301 1) audio visual production
2),3) Cyril John Schlosser
4) Communication Arts
5) 1973(U.S.A.)
6) yellow(PMS123)／orange(PMS165)／magenta
302 1) publishing
2),3) Hiroshi Manzen
4) Japan Scientific Societies Press
5) 1982(Japan)
303 1) building
2),3) Bob Swisher
4) Custom Builders, Inc.
6) brown
304 1) cobbler
2),3) Mo Lebowitz
4) Cobbler's bench
5) 1983(New York)
6) black
305 1) private symbol(photographer)
2),3) James Lienhart
4) Conrad Bailey Photography
5) (Chicago)
306 1) automobile (manufacturer)
2),3) Marty Neumeier
4) Clenet Coachworks
5) 1977(U.S.A.)
6) black
307 1) engineering company
2),3) Allan W.Miller
4) Corporacion Consultora
5) 1983(U.S.A.)
6) gray
308
2),3) Don Connelly
4) Chaney and Associates
5) 1980(U.S.A.)
6) gold
309
2),3) Stephan Kantscheff
4) Promischleno Stroitelstwo
5) 1971(Bulgaria)
310 1) chemical industry
2),3) Stephan Kantscheff
4) Chimconprect
5) 1983(Bulgaria)
311 1) theater
2),3) Stephan Kantscheff
4) Ancient Theater in Sofia
5) 1979(Bulgaria)
312 1) machine industry
2) Mark Topczewski／Frances Ullenberg
3) Ken Eichenbaum
4) Cross Company
5) 1981(Milwaukee)
6) blue green／gray
313 1) holding company
2),3) Eduard A.Canovas
5) 1973(Buenos Aires)
6) red
314 1) paint marketing company
2),3) James Lienhart
4) Color Communications,Inc.
5) (Chicago)

315 1) chamber of commerce
2),3) Hiroshi Manzen
4) The Canadian Chamber of Commerce in Japan
5) 1982(Japan)
6) DIC725
316
2),3) Milton Glaser
4) Inhilco
5) 1974(New York)
6) black／blue／red／yellow
317 1) building
2),3) João Carlos Cauduro／Ludovico Antonio Martno
4) Camargo Campos S.A.
5) 1977(São Paulo)
318 1) design studio
2),3) Rick Cusik
4) Rick Cusik Design
5) 1983(U.S.A.)
6) black
319 1) computer
2),3) Rolf Harder
4) Compu Design, Inc.
5) 1982(Montreal)
6) black or blue
320
2) Ronaldo Cutro
3) Cutro Associates, Inc.
4) Concord Enterprises
5) 1973(U.S.A.)
6) yellow ochre／black
321 1) food
2),3) Gary Ball
4) Console Foods, Inc.
5) 1983(U.S.A.)
6) light blue／dark blue
322 1) film company
2),3) Fernando Rión
4) Concord Films S.A.
5) 1977(Mexico)
6) orange
323 1) movie production
2),3) Jorge Sposari
4) Cañas y Flores S.A.
5) 1977(Buenos Aires)
6) black
324 1) investment firm
2) Mike Quon／David Rubin
3) Mike Quon
4) Colin Hochstin Company
5) 1977(New York)
6) brown
325 1) automobile parts(manufacturing)
2),3) Bob Swisher
4) C&H Auto Parts
5) black
326 1) art gallery
2),3) Stephan Kantscheff
4) Strasita
5) 1976(Bulgaria)
327 1) hotel
2),3) Tamás Ernö
4) Coop Hotel
5) 1983(Budapest)
6) dark brown
328 1) movie studio
2),3) Stephan Kantscheff
4) Sofia Film
5) 1970(Bulgaria)
329 1) information development
2),3) Burton Kramer
4) Centre Inn

5) 1979(Toronto)
6) green
330 1) concrete industry
2),3) Francesco Burcini
4) Calcestruzzi Centro Italia
5) 1972(Italy)
6) blue／orange
331 1) jeweller
2),3) Henry Steiner
4) Classic Jewellers, Ltd.
5) 1973(Hong Kong)
6) gold／silver
332 1) advertising agency
2),3) Richard Wittosch
4) C.K. & Associates
5) 1975(U.S.A.)
6) gray
333 1) geological survey
3) Yutaka Mitani
4) Chishitsu Keisoku
5) 1979(Japan)
334 1) architect
3) Hiroyasu Saijo
4) Cost Leader Co.,Ltd.
5) 1981(Japan)
335 1) ceramic industry
2),3) Alfredo de Santis
4) Ceramiche Musa
5) 1974(Rome)
336 1) museum
2),3) Robert L.Willis
4) The Children's Museum Indianapolis
5) 1973(U.S.A.)
6) orange
337 1) building
2),3) F.R.Esteban
4) Oxford Development Corporation
5) 1980(U.S.A.)
6) black
338 1) petroleum producer
2),3) J.Barton
4) Continental Petroleum
5) 1979(U.S.A.)
6) black
339
2) Ronald Cutro
3) Cutro Associates, Inc.
4) Continental Plaza
5) 1972(U.S.A.)
6) gold
340 1) textile product
2),3) Michio Ogura
4) Tokyo Young Brothers
5) 1979(Japan)
341
2),3) PVDI
4) Copersucar
5) 1976(Brasil)
342 1) construction
2),3) Charlotte Potts
4) Industrial and Commercial Property Construction
5) 1976(U.S.A.)
6) silver／black
343 1) broadcasting
2),3) Stephan Kantscheff
4) Samorowel
5) 1979(Bulgaria)
344 1) broadcasting(sports service)
3) Nikola Nikolov
4) Bulgarian T.V.
5) 1976(Bulgaria)

6) black/white
345 1) real estate
2) Mike Quon/S.Lewis
3) Mike Quon
4) Capital Planning Resources
5) 1974(New York)
6) brown
346 1) cosmetic
2),3) Fumio Koyoda
4) Max Co.,Ltd.
5) 1982(Japan)
347 1) insurance
2),3) Maria Mazzara
4) Central Security Insurance Company
5) 1980(U.S.A.)
6) blue/brown
348 1) photo studio
2),3) Silvio Gayton
4) Coronado Studios
5) 1981(U.S.A.)
6) dark blue/sky blue
349 1) machine industry
2) Mark Topczewski/Frances Ullenberg
3) Ken Eichenbaum
4) Cross and Trecker
5) 1981(Milwaukee)
6) brown/gray
350 1) metal industry
2),3) Buchan Tastan
4) Tuna Celik
5) 1982(Istanbul)
6) blue
351 1) movie
2),3) Fernando Medina
4) Cinetecnica
5) 1981(Madrid)
6) red/green
352 1) university
2),3) Don Nichols
4) State University of New York at Buffalo
5) 1977(New York)
6) black
353 1) electronics industry
2),3) Stephan Kantscheff
4) Electronics Association
5) 1982(Bulgaria)
354
2),3) Pietro Galli
4) Casa Treviso
5) 1970(Italy)
6) black
355 1) real estate(investment)
2),3) Robert Hargenhoffer
4) Creative Capital Corporation
5) (U.S.A.)
356 1) interior(selling)
2),3) Katsuichi Ito
4) Captain Cook Co.,Ltd.
5) 1974(Japan)
357 1) culture center
2),3) Tomás Vellvé
4) Mediterranian Culture Center
5) 1972(Barcelona)
6) black
358 1) computer
2),3) Milton Glaser
4) Children's Computer Workshop
5) 1982(New York)
6) red/blue/green

359 1) machine industry
2),3) Don Connelly
4) Crusader Equipment Inc.
5) 1973(U.S.A.)
6) red
360 1) government agency
2),3) Selahattin Sönmez
4) Turkish State Monopoly(GIN)
5) 1973(Istanbul)
6) blue
361 1) real estate
2),3) Masatoshi Shimokawa
4) CKG Inc.
5) 1975(Japan)
6) green
362 1) air conditioner
2) R.Naya/G.Romani/D.Soffientini/A.Ubertazzi
3) Environmental design center
4) Conditionarento Nord Italia
5) 1973(Italy)
6) red/green
363 1) newsmen national school
2),3) Rey Dacosta R.
4) Colegio Nacional de Periodistas
5) 1976(Venezuela)
6) dark blue
364 1) culture center
2),3) PVDI
4) Centro Nacional de Referência Cultural
5) 1976(Brazil)
365 1) private community club
2),3) Rey Dacosta R.
4) CR3(The Three Friends)
5) 1974(Venezuela)
6) black
366 1) travel agency
2),3) Othmar Motter
4) Reise-Club Rheintal
5) 1980(Austria)
6) black/white
367 1) valve manufacturer
2) F.R. Esteban
3) Jeff Piatt
4) Coupling Systems, Inc.
5) 1980(U.S.A.)
6) black
368 1) design
2),3) Joseph Churchward
4) Churchward International Typeface Co.
5) 1973(New Zealand)
6) blue
369
2),3) Milton Glaser
4) Children's Television Workshop
5) 1982(New York)
6) red/blue/green
370 1) broadcasting
3) Nikola Niholov
4) Bulgarian T.V.
5) 1977(Bulgaria)
6) black/white
371
2),3) PVDI
4) Dimelo Construções e Empreendimentos
5) 1976(Brazil)
372 1) furniture designer and

manufacturer
2),3) Rolf Harder
4) International Design and Woodcraft
5) 1978(Montreal)
6) black/brown
373
2),3) Terry Lesniewicz/Al Navarre
4) Dunbar Mechanical
5) 1972(U.S.A.)
374 1) industrial design studio
3) Carlo Malerba
4) Open Design
5) 1978(Italy)
6) black
375 1) foodstuff
2),3) Hideki Aoki
4) Daimaru Shokuhin
5) 1982(Japan)
376
2),3) Paul Ibou
4) Bouwonderneming D'Hulst
5) 1974(Belgium)
377 1) clothing store
2),3) Hiroko Ikemoto
4) Darumaya
5) 1980(Japan)
378 1) leather and shoes maker
2),3) Fernando Rión
4) Grupo Domit, S.A.
5) 1979(Mexico)
6) Pantone492
379 1) architect
3) Tytus Walczak
4) Przedsie Biorstwo Budowy Drogi Mostów
5) 1976(Poland)
6) black
380 1) gardening engineering
2) Akira Hirata
3) Akira Hirata/Hiroshi Mori
4) Daiichi Zoen Doboku Co., Ltd.
5) 1981(Japan)
381 1) holding company
2) Joe Vera
3) Joe Vera/Francisco Telez
4) Diblo S.A.
5) 1979(Mexico)
382
2),3) Silvio Gayton
4) Dired, Inc.
5) 1979(U.S.A.)
6) brown/black
383 1)investment broker
2),3) Allan W.Miller
4) Dillman+Danaher Investments
5) 1970(U.S.A.)
6) ochre
384 1) restaurant
2),3) Tamás Ernö
4) Duna-River Restaurant
5) 1983(Hungary)
6) dark blue
385 1) construction material
2),3) Franktišek Boban
4) Drefo Kombinat
5) 1975(Czechoslovakia)
386
2),3) Richard Wittosch
4) DuPage Power Wash, Inc.
5) 1980(U.S.A.)

6) bright blue
387 1) design festival
2),3) Akisato Ueda
4) 21st Century Association
5) 1982(Japan)
388 1) design studio
2),3) Burton Kramer
4) Design Dynamics, Ltd.
5) 1980(Canada)
6) brown
389 1) regional government
2),3) Ron Richards
4) Durham Regional Government
5) 1974(Canada)
6) blue
390
2),3) Frutiger Adrian
4) CGE-Distribution
5) 1977(France)
6) black
391 1) consulting Co.
2),3) Ernesto Lehfeld
4) Dinamica, S.A.
5) 1975(Mexico)
6) PMS 158
392 1) electric appliance
2),3) Ernesto Lehfeld
4) Duratronic, S.A.
5) 1980(Mexico)
6) PMS 292
393 1) design studio
2),3) Gustavo Gomez-Casallas/Rodrigo Fernandez
4) Diseño
5) 1977(Colombia)
6) red
394 1) industry product
2),3) Gustavo Gomez-Casallas/Michel Vandame/Rodrigo Fernandez
4) Dinmar-Distribuidores de Productos del Mar
5) 1980(Colombia)
6) blue
395 1) education
2),3) Gustavo Gomez-Casallas/Rodrigo Fernandez
4) Formas Didacticas
5) 1981(Colombia)
6) green
396 1) building material market
2),3) Walter Hergenröther
4) Building Material R.De Eccher
5) 1976(Italy)
6) dark blue/red/orange
397 1) interior
3) Shigetoshi Shibata
4) Yoshinoto
5) (Japan)
398
2),3) Francesco Burcini
4) Dolciaria San Gemini
5) 1982(Italy)
6) brown/beige
399 1) building material(timber)
2),3) Franktisek Boban
4) Drevo Industria
5) 1973(Czechoslovakia)
400 1) design studio
2) Gottschalk+Ash International

Index to Contained Works

3) Stuart Ash
4) D.I. Design and Development, Ltd.
5) 1972(Toronto)

401 1) private symbol
3) Nikola Nikolov
4) Danail Ignatov
5) 1979(Bulgaria)
6) black/white

402 1) communication
2),3) Conrad E.Angone
4) David Kalbach & Associates
5) 1974(Los Angeles)
6) deep blue

403 1) county council
3) Kenneth Hollick
4) Derbyshire County Council
5) 1975(London)
6) mauve

404 1) private symbol(engineer)
2),3) Denise Spaulding
4) David Osborne
5) 1980(U.S.A.)
6) gray

405 1) plumber
2),3) Terry Lesniewicz/Al Navarre
4) Duquette Plumbing
5) 1977(U.S.A.)

406 1) film production company
2),3) Mike Quon
4) Devi Productions
5) 1971(New York)
6) blue

407 1) sport(association)
2),3) Stephan Kantscheff
4) Dunav
5) 1980(Bulgaria)

408 1) photographic studio
2),3) Manfred Korten
4) Doris Reinemann Fotostudio Solingen
5) 1983(West Germany)
6) black

409 1) metal stamping -forming
2),3) Cyril John Schlosser
4) Division Stampings, Inc.
5) 1972(U.S.A.)
6) black/red(PMS 485)

410 1) meat packer
2) John DiGianni
3) Gianninoto Associates,Inc.
4) Dak Foods, Inc.
5) 1980(U.S.A.)
6) red/blue

411 1) foundation
2),3) Ernesto Lehfeld
4) UNAM-Cultural and Artistic Foundation
5) 1975(Mexico)
6) PMS 464

412 1) designers' association
2),3) Ernesto Lehfeld
4) Mexico Designers' Association
5) 1972(Mexico)
6) PMS 300

413 1) costume design
2),3) Osamu Furumura
4) Dana
5) 1980(Japan)

414 1) general store
2) Katsuhiko Yasuda
3) Katsuichi Ito
4) Doit Co.,Ltd.
5) 1980(Japan)
6) orange

415 1) theatre
2),3) Herbert Binneweg
4) Antwerp Theatre & Concert Hall
5) 1979(Belgium)
6) black

416 1) chemical industry
2),3) Stephan Kantscheff
4) Dewnja
5) 1974(Bulgaria)

417 1) food product
2) John Follis
3) Jean-Claude Muller
4) Dharmala
5) 1981(U.S.A.)
6) black

418
2),3) Shin'ich Takahara
4) Hokkaido Doral
5) 1982(Japan)

419 1) chemical industry
3) Matjaž Bertonceli
4) Yugocryl Liubliana
5) 1972(Yugoslavia)
6) sienna

420 1) mode selling
2),3) Oanh Pham-Phu
4) Dismero Mode Vertrieb GmbH
5) 1983(West Germany)
6) yellow/blue/red

421 1) drilling company
2),3) Ernesto Lehfeld
4) Dril de Mexico,S.A.
5) 1971(Mexico)
6) PMS 404/PMS 300

422 1) electric work
2),3) Masahiro Abe
4) Daiwa Electric Work Co., Ltd.
5) 1981(Japan)
6) DIC 162

423 1) language teaching
2),3) Marchionni Carlo
4) Didaktica
5) 1977(Italy)
6) maroon

424 1) Private Symbol (photographer)
2),3) Pat Taylor
4) Dal Bayles
5) 1973(U.S.A.)
6) black

425 1) publishing
2) Eleonora Turlakova
3) Christo Alexiev
4) Magazine "Woman Today"
5) 1981(Bulgaria)
6) black

426 1) leather(manufacturing)
2),3) Marchionni Carlo
4) Dascucci Pelletteria
5) 1978(Italy)
6) maroon

427 1) movie production
2),3) Jorge Sposari
4) Del Plata Distribuidores
5) 1976(Argentina)

428 1) political institute
2),3) Ernesto Lehfeld
4) Documentacion Politica A. G.
5) 1978(Mexico)
6) PMS 369

429 1) jewelry manufacture
2),3) Giovanni Brunazzi
4) David Rossi
5) 1970(Italy)
6) gold

430 1) transport
2),3) Francesco Burcini
4) Dinamica Umbra
5) 1976(Italy)
6) blue

431
2),3) Stephan Kantscheff
4) DDD
5) 1970(Bulgaria)

432
2),3) Don Young
4) Elite Circuits
5) 1978(U.S.A.)

433 1) sculptors meeting
2),3) Felix Beltran
4) Encuentro de Escultores
5) 1978(Mexico)
6) black

434 1) merchants association
2),3) Vasco Ceccon
4) Association des Commercants de Ste-Agathe
5) 1976(Montreal)
6) red

435
2),3) Ettore Vitale
4) Efibanca
5) 1977(Rome)

436 1) glass industry
2),3) Walter Hergenröther
4) Edil Glas Production Co.
5) 1978(Italy)
6) brown/yellow

437
2),3) R. Roger Remington
4) Econ Technologies
5) 1975(New York)
6) red

438
2),3) Armin Vogt
4) Edwin Vogt Partner AG
5) 1982(Switzerland)
6) Pantone 300

439
2),3) Tracy Turner
4) Ergometrix Office Systems, Inc.
5) 1978(New York)
6) blue

440 1) paper-manufacturing
3) Paul Ibou
4) Epacar Papier
5) 1977(Belgium)

441 1) clothing
2) Joe Vera
3) Francisco Tellez/Joe Vera
4) Emmanuelle
5) 1979(Mexico)

442 1) electric machinery
2),3) Stephan Kantscheff
4) Ministerium für Electronik und Electoteknik
5) 1971(Bulgaria)

443
3) Hugo Arape
4) Ecopex

5) 1977(France)
6) blue

444 1) hotel
2),3) Stephan Kantscheff
4) Europa
5) 1976(Bulgaria)

445 1) medicine (manufacturing)
2),3) Kazuo Tanaka
4) Torii & Co.,Ltd.
5) 1977(Japan)
6) CF 253/DIC 478

446 1) publishing
3) Sumio Hasegawa
4) Izerusha
5) 1972(Japan)

447 1) distribution
2) Hideto Suzuki
3) Shigo Yamaguchi/Masaki Furuta
4) Early Bird Co.,Ltd.
5) 1983(Japan)

448 1) public relations
2),3) Bill Bundzak
4) Earl Lyon Inc.
5) 1981(New York)
6) black

449 1) publishing
3) Paul Ibou
4) Esco Books
5) 1978(Belgium)

450 1) engineering
2),3) Jack Evans
4) Engineering Concepts
5) (U.S.A.)

451 1) national comittee
2),3) Ettore Vitale
4) ENEA-Comitato Nazionale
5) 1982(Rome)

452 1) community
2),3) Dieter Urban
4) European Community
5) 1973(Brussels)

453 1) electric machinery(manufacturing)
2),3) Elias Garcia Benavides
4) ERCOA-Electric Machinery Production Company
5) 1975(Spain)
6) black

454
2) Jack Weiss
3) Diana Lifton
4) Excelsior
5) 1980(U.S.A.)
6) black/gray

455 1) electronuclear industry
2),3) Giovanni Brunazzi
4) Elettronucleare Italiana
5) 1973(Italy)

456 1) service
2),3) Ernst Roch
4) Exposervice, Inc.
5) 1979(Montreal)

457 1) restaurant(fast food)
2),3) Marty Neumeier
4) Eatz
5) 1982(U.S.A.)
6) red

458 1) electronics industry
2),3) Rainer Strempel
4) Electronic-Data-Processing Corp.
5) 1970(West Germany)

459
2) Michael J.Rassell
3) Sylvia Sewell
4) Elf Products
5) 1981(London)
6) green
460 1) bank
2) Barbara Bowlend
3) David Leigh
4) East River Savings Bank
5) 1970(New York)
6) blue
461 1)professional teaching aid
2),3) David Leigh
4) Educational Solutions,Inc.
5) 1973(New York)
6) red
462 1) printing
2),3) Herbert Wenn
4) Emhart Offset-Printing
5) 1980(West Germany)
6) blue
463 1) touring
2),3) Alfredo de Santis
4) Ediltur
5) 1975(Rome)
464 1) chemical industry
2) Laszlo Lendvai
3) Erno Sara
4) Chemical Industry
5) 1983(Budapest)
6) dark green
465
2),3) Steve Sheldon
4) E-Z Enterprises
5) 1981(U.S.A.)
6) blue
466 1) electonics industry
2),3) Maria Mazzara
4) Electron Optics
5) 1975(U.S.A.)
6) dark blue/light blue
467 1) publishing
2),3) Sonja Wunderlich
4) Edition Leipzing
5) 1975(East Germany)
6) black
468 1) design studio
2),3) Scott Engen
4) Engen/Graphic USA
5) 1977(U.S.A.)
6) black/red
469 1) exhibition(art)
3) Ivan Dvorsak
5) 1980(Yugoslavia)
6) black
470 1) insurance firm
2),3) James Lienhart
4) Ellerman Companies, Inc.
5) (Chicago)
471 1) research
institute(environment)
2),3) Shigeo Katsuoka
4) Anzenkogaku Kenkyujo
5) 1975(Japan)
6) green(DIC 131)
472 1) municipality
2),3) Rainer Strempel
4) Municipality Essen
5) 1973(West Germany)
473 1) publishing
2),3) Gert Wunderlich
4) Edition Leipzig
5) 1975(East Germany)
6) black

474 1) municipality
2),3) Thomas Starr
4) City of New Rochelle
5) 1976(U.S.A.)
6) green
475 1) administration study
2),3) Morfos Diseño S.C.
4) EDAC-Estudios de
Administración Aplicada
5) 1983(Mexico)
6) light brown
476 1) shop
2) Júlia Nemes
3) Erno Sara
4) Ezermester
5) 1981(Budapest)
6) black
477
2),3) Massimo Dradi
4) Ecolco
5) 1974(Italy)
6) black
478 1) music festival
2),3) David Gibbs
4) Eastern Music Festival
5) 1978(U.S.A.)
6) reddish brown
479 1) university
2),3) Don Nichols
4) State University of New
York
5) 1973(New York)
6) red/orange/purple
480 1) furniture
2),3) Harry Murphy
4) Environmental Products
5) 1972(U.S.A.)
6) black/white
481 1) computer program
firm
2),3) Mike Quon
4) Executive Systems+
Programming
5) 1972(New York)
6) blue
482 1) computer company
2),3) Jean-Cleaude Muller
4) FINDEX
5) 1978(U.S.A.)
6) red(PMS 032)
483 1) association
(photographers)
3) Ivan Dvorsak
4) Fotoklub Maribor
5) 1975(Yugoslavia)
6) black
484 1) precision industry
2),3) Makoto Yoshida
4) Fuji Seiko Co.,Ltd.
5) 1981(Japan)
6) blue/purple(DIC 223)
485 1) electric and telephone
installation
3) A.G. Fronzoni
4) Finaldi
5) 1975(Milano)
6) black
486 1) public transport
2) R.Nava/D.Soffientini/A.
Ubertazzi
3) Da Centro per il Disegno
Ambientale
4) Frigerio
5) 1983(Italy)
6) green

487 1) smoking products
maker
2) Masamitsu Komatsubara
3) Ikuo Masubuchi
4) Terasaki Kogyo Co.,Ltd.
5) 1982(Japan)
488 1) bank
3) Wim Crouwel
4),Friesland Bank
5) 1973(Amsterdam)
6) black
489 1) foundation of
development of plastic art
2) Jacek Walczak
3) Jaroslaw Jasinski
4) Ministerstwo Kultury sztuići
5) 1983(Warszawa)
6) umber
490 1) electric
machinery(production)
3) Carlo Malerba
4) Federal Cei Spa
5) 1976(Italy)
491 1) food(manufacturing)
2),3) Aldo Novarese
4) Ferrero Chocolata
5) (Italy)
6) red
492 1) landscape gardening
2),3) Hiro Terao
4) Fuji-Landscape Co.,Ltd.
5) 1983(Japan)
6) green(DIC 214)/gray(DIC
546)
493 1) foundation
2),3) George Tscherny
4) Fidelity Group of Funds
5) 1979(New York)
494 1) agriculture
2) João Carlos Cauduro/
Ludovico Antonio Martino
4) Fujiwara Hisato SA
5) 1971(São Paulo)
495 1) building company
2),3) Othmar Motter
4) Gebrüder Feierle Hochbau
-Unternehmung
5) 1982(Austria)
6) black/white
496 1) trading
2),3) Jaime Gutierrez Lega
4) FRESPO-Fresas de
Exportacion
5) 1977(Bogota)
6) terracotta
497 1) petroleum
3) Paul Ibou
4) Frisol Nederland
5) 1981(Belgium)
498 1) airlines company
2),3) Saul Bass
4) Frontier Airlines
5) 1977(Los Angeles)
499 1) knitwear/tailoring
2) R.Nava/G.Romani/D.
Soffientini/A.Ubertazzi
3) Da Centro Per Il Disegno
Ambientale
4) Famos
5) 1976(Italy)
6) blue
500 1) fixtual fund company
2) Thomas Ohmer
3) Carl Seltzer
4) The Growth Fund of

America
5) 1976(Los Angeles)
6) green
501 1) transport
2),3) Shin'ichi Takahara
4) Fuji Kyuso
5) 1978(Japan)
502 1) bathing
material(manufacturing)
2),3) Hidemichi Yamao
4) Fresser-Honpo
5) 1983(Japan)
503 1) construction
2),3) Yasaburo Kuwayama
4) Fujisawa Construction
5) 1983(Japan)
504 1) conglomerate
2),3) Ray Engle
4) Flagg Industries,Inc.
5) 1972(Los Angeles)
6) purple/blue/magenta
505
2) Toshio Goto
3) Hiroshi Shibuya
4) Fukumi Group
5) 1979(Japan)
6) green/blue
506 1) textile industry
2),3) Stephan Kantscheff
4) Bulgaria Probdif
5) 1982(Bulgaria)
507 1) publissing
2),3) Lanny Sommese
4) Leisure Press"Fitness
America" Series
5) 1975(U.S.A.)
6) blue/white
508 1) advertising agency
2),3) Oanh Pham-Phu
4) Fischer Advertising
5) 1970(München)
6) red
509 1) book(selling)
3) Koichi Mizuno
4) Nippon Family Book K.K.
5) 1978(Japan)
510 1) lease(vending machine)
2),3) Shigeo Katsuoka
4) Fuji Vending Co.
5) 1978(Japan)
6) orange(DIC 160)
511 1) machine industry
2),3) Beppe Benenti
4) Fratelli Caudera
5) 1979(Italy)
6) green/gray
512 1) computer service
2),3) Herbert Wenn
4) Follmann GmbH
5) 1982(West Germany)
6) black/white
513 1) financial group
2),3) Guillermo Gonzalez Ruiz
4) Financiera Faciema
5) 1975(Buenos Aires)
6) green/blue
514 1) design studio
2),3) Burhan Tastan
4) Fon Graphic
5) 1977(Istanbul)
6) blue
515 1) geological consultant
2) John Follis
3) Joe Stoddard
4) Converse Davis Dixon

5) 1977(Los Angeles)
6) brown
516 1) printed matter(catalogue)
2) Shunji Niinomi
3) Tetsuharu Mabuchi
4) Toyota Jidosha
5) 1978(Japan)
517 1) human relations company
2),3) Carlos Rolando
4) Factor Humano
5) 1974(Barcelona)
6) black/white
518 1) trade(fruit)
2),3) Adam Moltke
4) Frimex Fruit Importers
5) 1983(Denmark)
6) green/red
519 1) bank
3) Fred E.Denzler
4) First National Bank of Libertyville
5) 1971(U.S.A.)
6) blue/green
520 1) photographic course
2),3) Kazuo Ono
4) Fuji Film Co.,Ltd.
5) 1975(Japan)
521 1) textile industry
2),3) Christof Gassner
4) Frankische Gobelin
5) 1980(Frankfurt)
6) black
522 1) industrial plant operator
2),3) David Leigh
4) Fairlawn Industries,Inc.
5) 1970(New York)
6) violet
523 1) subway
2),3) Fumio Koyoda
4) Fukuoka City
5) 1979(Japan)
524 1) landscape gardening
2) Calvin Woo
3) Calvin Woo/Mike Whalen
4) Fry & Stone Associates
5) 1983(U.S.A.)
6) dark green
525
3) Fred E.Denzler
4) Form Corporation
5) 1970(U.S.A.)
6) olive green/black
526
2),3) Don Davis
4) Thymos Corp.
5) 1975(U.S.A.)
6) black
527 1) automotive repair factory
2) Atsutaka Chono
3) Hideshi Takahashi
4) Futatsuka Jidosha
5) 1982(Japan)
528 1) glass and Christmas tree decoration
2) Kazimierz Mann
3) Jarostaw Jasinski
4) P.FINDERA
5) 1970(Warszawa)
6) black
529 1) automotive industry
3) Tytus Walczak
4) Automotive factory

Warszawa
5) 1980(Warszawa)
6) black
530 1) private symbol(formative artist)
2),3) Franktisěk Boban
5) 1973(Czechoslovakia)
531 1) music(orchestra)
2),3) Gustavo Gomez -Casallas/Rodrigo Fernandez
4) Orquesta Filarmonica
5) 1982(Colombia)
6) blue
532 1) festival
2),3) Stephan Kantscheff
5) (Bulgaria)
533 1) self-governing council
3) Koichi Mizuno
4) Fujinodai Danchi Jichikai
5) 1972(Japan)
534 1) music festival
2),3) Stephan Kantscheff
4) Black Sea Music Festival
5) 1970(Bulgaria)
535 1) symposium
2),3) Stephan Kantscheff
4) Photo Vacantion Sosopol
5) 1982(Bulgaria)
536 1) union
2),3) Joe Dieter
4) The Fiber Union
5) 1982(U.S.A.)
6) brown
537 1) music(orchestra)
2),3) Stephan Kantscheff
4) Sofia Philharmonia
5) 1978(Bulgaria)
538 1) design studio
2),3) Masaki Fukuda
4) Fukuda Design Studio
5) 1981(Japan)
539 1)festival
3) Kenneth Hollick
4) Fanfare for Europe
5) 1973(London)
6) black
540 1) holding company
2),3) Miani Luigi/Redaelli Guido
4) Finitaliana
5) 1974(Milano)
6) brown
541 1) ceramics manufacturing
3) Szekeres Istvan
4) FIM
5) 1973(Budapest)
6) blue
542 1) film production company
2),3) Joe Vera
4) FORO 70
5) 1973(Mexico)
6) black/silver
543 1) medicine (manufacturing)
2) Mitsuo Ishida
3) Tamami Sato
4) Fujikawa
5) 1971(Japan)
544 1) broadcasting
2) Jack Evans
3) Unigraphics, Inc.
4) Gulf Broadcast Gruop
5) 1980(U.S.A.)
6) dark blue

545 1) typography
2),3) Alfredo de Santis
4) G.E.A.P.
5) 1978(Rome)
546
2) Ken Eichenbaum
3) Doris Stein
4) Golden Guernsey Dairy
5) 1975(U.S.A.)
6) magenta/orange
547 1) ski maker
2) Yuji Kawarabayashi
3) Akisato Ueda
4) GTO Co., Ltd.
5) 1975(Japan)
548 1) electric part
2) Nobuyuki Hagiwara
3) Fumio Koyoda
4) Matsushita Electric Works, Ltd.
5) 1981(Japan)
549 1) bank
2),3) James Lienhart
4) Gary National Bank
5) (Chicago)
550 1) machine industry
2),3) Walter Hergenröther
4) Mechanische Werkstätte
5) 1980(Italy)
6) black/red
551 1) association(graphic design)
2),3) Kazuo Kishimoto
4) Japan Graphic Designer Association
5) (Japan)
552 1) bus construction
2) R.Nava/D.Soffientini/A. Ubertazzi
3) Da Centro Per Il Disegno Arbientale
4) Gammabus
5) 1981(Italy)
6) blue
553 1) textile product
2) Yoshiaki Nakano
3) Akira Hirata
4) World Co.,Ltd.
5) 1979(Japan)
6) Pantone 185c
554 1) building management
2),3) Manfred Korten
4) Grah Hausverwaltungen
5) 1983(West Germany)
6) black
555 1) chemical industry
2),3) Tracy Turner
4) Gulf States Chemical Co.
5) 1980(New York)
6) gray/blue
556
2),3) Heinz Waibl
4) Gasdarotto SPA
5) 1971(Milano)
557 1) marketing
2) Sudarshan Dheer
3) Prakash Patil
4) Good Value Marketing Co., Ltd.
5) 1979(Bombay)
6) red/blue
558 1) publishing
2),3) Silvio Gayton
4) The Guiness Record Group, Inc.

5) 1979(U.S.A.)
6) silver/light gray
559
2),3) Gavin Healey
4) Peter Green
5) 1975(London)
6) red/green
560
2),3) Charles M.Mosco
4) Granite State Credit Union
5) 1983(New York)
6) green
561 1) electronics
2) Peter Christensen
3) Burkhalter Marc
4) Gretag AG
5) 1982(Switzerland)
6) blue
562 1) furniture
2),3) Oanh Pham-Phu
4) Deutscher Möbel Verbund Handels GmbH
5) 1978(München)
6) brown/black
563 1) holding company
2),3) Jack Evans
4) Gulf Life Holding Company
5) (U.S.A.)
564 1) antique
2),3) Othmar Motter
4) Antiquariat GERBER
5) 1981(Austria)
565 1) restaurant
2),3) Umberto Facchini
4) Goppion Caffe
5) 1970(Italy)
6) black
566 1)festival
2),3) Stan Brod
4) Gilligan Election Campaign
5) 1970(U.S.A.)
6) red/white/blue
567 1) private symbol
2),3) Terry Lesniewicz/Al Navarre
4) Gordon Grant
5) 1979(U.S.A.)
568 1) architect
2),3) Allan W.Miller
4) Group Five Architects
5) 1977(U.S.A.)
6) dark blue
569 1) cosmetic
2),3) Fumio Koyoda
4) Max Co.,Ltd.
5) 1983(Japan)
570 1) indoor swimming pool
3) Rosmarie Tissi
4) Geminde Geroldswil
5) 1976(Zürich)
6) blue/yellow
571 1) cybernetic
2),3) Morfos Diseño
4) GREBSA Cibernética,S.A.
5) 1981(Mexico)
6) blue
572 1) plastic industry
2),3) Burton Kramer
4) Gentil Plastics,Ltd.
5) 1971(Toronto)
6) orange
573
2),3) Burton Kramer
4) Glassworks
5) 1980(Toronto)

6) blue/green
574 1) electronics
2),3) Hans Hartzheim
4) Gehrkens Electrotechniek
5) 1978(Hague)
6) blue
575 1) theatre
2),3) Joseph Boggs
4) Grand Dinner Theater
5) 1982(U.S.A.)
6) red/yellow/blue/green
576 1) forestry
3) Ivan Dvoršak
4) Gozdno Gospodarsvo Novo
Mestro
5) 1976(Yugoslavia)
6) green
577 1) hospital
2),3) Shin Ikeda
4) Kashiwaba Neuro-surgery
5) 1982(Japan)
6) blue(Toyo CF5228)
578 1) hospital
2),3) Edward Hughes
4) The Glenbrook Hospital
5) 1974(U.S.A.)
6) orange
579 1) hospital
2),3) Calvin Woo
4) Grossmont Hospital
5) 1973(U.S.A.)
6) gold
580 1) accordion
2),3) Francesco Brucini
4) Grasselli
5) 1979(Italy)
6) violet
581 1) pub
2),3) Toshiyasu Nambu
4) Karubotei
5) 1977(Japan)
582
2),3) Armin Vogt
4) Grafothek
5) 1974(Switzerland)
6) red(Pantone032)/black
583 1) manufacturing
2),3) Rick Cartledge
4) Global Marine Products,Ltd.
5) 1981(Canada)
6) red
584 1) travel agency
2),3) Moriyoshi Ijima
4) Gyro Co.,Ltd.
5) 1983(Japan)
585 1) publishing
2),3) Makoto Yoshida
4) Green Arrow Shuppansha
5) 1983(Japan)
6) golden red/green
586 1) vinyl
bag(manufacturing)
2) Katsumi Nagata/Yasaburo
Kuwayama
3) Yasaburo Kuwayama/Ikuo
Masubuchi
4) Green Chemical
5) 1974(Japan)
6) blue/green
587 1) musical group
2),3) Peter Kneebone
4) Grosvenor Ensemble
5) 1970(Paris)
6) black
588 1) construction

2),3) Steve Shelden
4) G & F Construction Co.
5) 1979(U.S.A.)
6) gray
589 1) leasing company
2),3) Ray R. Dacosta
4) Gruas Guanipa
5) 1982(Caracas)
590 1) private
symbol(decorator)
2),3) Paul Ibou
4) Guy Lamoral
5) 1970(Belgium)
591 1) art gallery
2),3) Franktisěk Boban
4) Oclesna Galleria
5) 1975(Czechoslovakia)
592 1) real estate
2) Akira Hirata
3) Akira Hirata/Hiroshi Tada
4) Nichimo Co.,Ltd.
5) 1979(Japan)
6) Pantone green
593 1) university
2),3) Don Nichols
4) State University of New
York
5) 1971(New York)
6) black
594 1) clothing
2),3) Stephan Kantscheff
4) Septembri
5) 1982(Bulgaria)
595
2) Kenneth R.Cooke
3) Eric Scott
4) Murjani International,Ltd.
5) (New York)
596 1) sounding
machine(selling)
2),3) Rey R. Dacosta
4) Giro 4
5) 1978(Caracas)
6) blue
597 1) advertising
3) Carlo Malerba
4) Grupo Pubblicitario Bustino
5) 1981(Italy)
598 1) computer(data
processing)
2),3) Claudio Doveri
4) General Data Processing
5) 1975(Milano)
6) amaranth
599 1) private symbol
2),3) David Leigh
4) Gerald E.Thomas
5) 1973(New York)
6) brown
600 1) textile industry
2),3) Philip Gips
4) General Felt Industries
5) 1978(New York)
6) black
601 1) hospital
2) Richard Yeager
3) Richard Yeager/Mike
Chapman
4) Gaudenzia-Drug
Rehabilitation Center
5) 1971(U.S.A.)
6) black
602 1) confectionary
2) Akira Hirata
3) Akira Hirata/Hironobu

Yanagida
4) Ginso Co.,Ltd.
5) 1979(Japan)
6) Pantone 339c
603
2) Ann Bodlund
3) Hans Kündig
4) Guldsmedjernas Inköps AB
5) 1981(Sweden)
6) black
604 1) consulting firm
corporate for employee relation
2),3) GMB Associates
4) 1981(U.S.A.)
605
2),3) Ernesto Lehfeld
4) Nuestro Gran Sueno,S.A.
5) 1983(Mexico)
6) PMS 169
606 1) industry
2),3) Kazuo Kishimoto
4) Ryukyu Golex Co.,Ltd.
5) (Japan)
607
2),3) Dicken Castro
4) Grupo Radial Colombiano
5) 1981(Colombia)
6) black/red
608 1) sportscar racing team
2) Thomas Ohmer
3) Bruce Dobson
4) Great Western Racing
5) 1979(Los Angeles)
6) red
609 1) office machine and
furniture
2),3) Othmar Motter
4) Ganahl
5) 1973(Austria)
610 1) construction
2),3) Don Davis
4) Golden Bros.
5) 1977(U.S.A.)
6) gray
611 1) art gallery
2),3) Silvio Gayton
4) Desk Gallery,Inc.
5) 1981(U.S.A.)
6) beige/dark brown
612 1) painting material
2) Hiroyasu Inouchi
3) Akisato Ueda
4) Kansai Paint Co.,Ltd.
5) 1974(Japan)
613 1) design studio
2),3) Morteza Momayez
4) "Form" Graphic Studio
5) 1972(Teheran)
614 1) hotel
3) Yoshinori Mori
4) Kanazawa New Grand Hotel
5) 1972(Japan)
615 1) public relations
company
3) Kenneth Hollick
4) Geoffrey Tucker
5) 1971(London)
6) white(embossed)
616 1) private
symbol(graphic designer)
2),3) Gun Larson
4) Gun Larson
5) 1971(Sweden)
6) black
617 1) printing

2) Soichi Saito
3) Katsuichi Ito
4) Hokushin Printing Co.,Ltd.
5) 1982(Japan)
618 1) interior (furniture
making)
2) Morócz István
3) Ernó Sára
4) Hindermann Seat Furniture
5) 1974(Budapest)
619 1) hotel
2),3) Felix Beltran
4) Hotel Henequen
5) 1975(Mexico)
6) deep green
620
2),3) Chermayeff & Geismar
Associates
4) Halaby International
Corporation
5) (U.S.A.)
6) blue/red
621
2),3) Chermayeff & Geismar
Associates
4) Hechinger Company
5) (U.S.A.)
6) blue
622 1) sport(facilities)
2) Monica Brown/Stan Brod
3) Stan Brod
4) Health Careers of Ohio
5) 1975(U.S.A.)
6) dark blue
623 1) hospital
2) Robert P.Gersin
3) Robert P.Gersin/Abner
Gutierrez
4) Hackensack Medical Center
5) 1982(New York)
6) green
624 1) insurance
2),3) Dieter Urban
4) Hessen-Nassawische
Versicherung Wiesbaben
5) 1981(Brussels)
625 1) supermarket
2),3) Stephan Kantscheff
4) Halli
5) 1972(Bulgaria)
626 1) electrical machinery
2),3) Robert Hargenhoffer
4) Hipertonicks Co.
5) (U.S.A.)
627
2),3) Paul Ibou
4) Drukkerij Tengrootenhuysen
5) 1982(Belgium)
628
2),3) Don Young
4) Hallmark Circuits
5) 1979(U.S.A.)
629 1) shopping cernter
2),3) Burton Kramer
4) Hallmark Hornepayne Town
Centre
5) 1978(Toronto)
6) red/orange
630
2),3) Burton Kramer
4) Hallmark Hotels, Ltd.
5) 1977(Toronto)
6) blue
631 1) hotel
2),3) Hidemichi Yamao

4) Hotel Sogo Palace
5) 1982(Japan)
632
2) Stan Brod/Monica Brown
3) Stan Brod
4) Cincinnati Health Careers
5) 1974(U.S.A.)
6) dark blue
633
3) Michael Herold
5) 1979(West Germany)
6) blue
634
2),3) Henry Steiner
4) The Hong Kong Land Co.,
Ltd.
5) 1970(Hong Kong)
6) black/white
635 1) alcoholic
liquor(selling)
2) Takao Sasaki
3) Takao Sasaki/Yutaka Mitani
4) Hiraki
5) 1982(Japan)
636 1) design studio
2),3) Ken'ichi Hirose
4) Ken'ichi Hirose's Design
Office
5) 1974(Japan)
6)gray
637 1) textile
2),3) Masahiro Abe
4) Hagiwara Co.,Ltd.
5) 1980(Japan)
6) orange (DIC163)
638 1) freezer industry
2),3) Koichi Watanabe
4) Hirota
5) 1976
639 2),3) Burton Kramer
4) Heron Gate Mall
5) 1981(Toronto)
6) orange
640 1) construction
2),3) Herbert Wenn
4) Walter Horn Architects
5) 1977(West Germany)
6) black/white
641 1) interior
3) Yoneo Jinbo
4) Honda Curtain
5) 1977(Japan)
642 1) glass industry
2) Keith Murgatroyd
3) Tony Forster
4) Hammerplast Ag.
5) 1975(Manchester)
6) black
643 1) construction
2) Keith Murgatroyd
3) Tony Forster
4) J.W.Haynes & Sons, Ltd.
5) 1974(Manchester)
6) olive green
644
2),3) Don Connelly
4) Hirt Realty
5) 1977(U.S.A.)
6) dark blue
645 1) communication
2),3) Don Connelly
4) Hobis Telephone Systems
5) 1983(U.S.A.)
6) black

646
2),3) Ruut Van Den Hoed
4) Hutzler
5) 1974(U.S.A.)
6) black
647 1) perfume(making)
3) G.Edwards
4) Ebesa
5) 1977(Mexico)
6) brown
648 1) printing
2),3) Lanny Sommese
4) Himes Printing Co.
5) 1975(U.S.A.)
6) blue/white
649 1) metalworking industry
2),3) Ernst Roch
4) Henderson Steel
Construction
5) 1974(Montreal)
650 1) coating material
2),3) George McGinnis
4) Harrad Paint Company
5) 1982(New York)
651 1) food(supply)
2),3) Lanny Sommese
4) Hoags Catering
5) 1982(U.S.A.)
6) black/white
652 1) motive power
2),3) Terry Lesniewicz/Al
Navarre
4) Hydro Energy System
5) 1973(U.S.A.)
653 1) farming
2),3) István Szekeres
4) Agroinform
5) 1976(Budapest)
654 1) interior(wig)
2),3) Akisato Ueda
4) Hi Brand
5) 1973(Japan)
655
2),3) Paul Ibou
4) Herman Carpentier
5) 1982(Belgium)
656 1) private
symbol(furniture designer)
2),3) Ernesto Lehfeld
4) Horacio Duran
5) 1971(Mexico)
6) PMS153
657 1) consultant(financial)
2),3) James Lienhart
4) Head/Ellerman,Inc.
5) (Chicago)
658 1) electrical machinery
2),3) Manfred Wutke
4) Hecker Electronics
5) 1976(West Germany)
6) blue/red
659 1) interior shop
2),3) Akisato Ueda
4) Interior Hasegawa
5) 1974(Japan)
660 1) hotel
2),3) Julien Van Der Wal
4) Hotel Metropole
5) 1982(Geneve)
661
2),3) Hans Kündig
4) Hjalmar Pettersson
5) 1975(Sweden)
6) black

662
3) Michael Herold
5) 1983(West Germany)
6) brown
663 1) metallurgy
2),3) Jose Luis Aguirre
4) Herreria Rodriguez
5) 1982(Rome)
6) black
664
2),3) Oanh Pham-Phu
4) Hans Schulz
5) 1974(München)
6) red
665
2) Sture Lindholm
3) Kurt Netzler
4) C.G.Hallbergs/
Guldsmedsaktiebolag
5) 1976(Sweden)
6) dark green
666 1) construction
2) Keith Murgatroyd
3) Tony Forster
4) Richard Hemingway &
Partners
5) 1982(Manchester)
6) orange
667 1) medicine(producing)
2) Jack Weiss
3) Randi Robin
4) Hollister,Inc.
5) 1979(U.S.A.)
6) red(PMS186)
668
2) Stankowski/Duschek
3) Anton Stankowski
4) Landesgartenschau
Schwäbisch Hall
5) 1982(West Germany)
669 1) interior(furniture)
2),3) Cyril John Schlosser
4) Honor Industries, Inc.
5) 1971(U.S.A.)
6) blue(PMS285)
670 1) sport(bowling center)
2),3) Shuji Torigoe
4) Homare Bowling Center
5) 1972(Japan)
671 1) interior(shop)
2),3) Yasaburo Kuwayama
4) Honma Interior
5) 1983(Japan)
6) orange
672 1) printing
2),3) Cyril John Schlosser
4) Hart Press
5) 1971(U.S.A.)
6) blue(PMS285)
673 1) health studio
2) Tsuyokatsu Kudo
3) Tsuyokatsu Kudo/Hiroshi
Nishino
4) Sun Sports Club Co.,Ltd.
5) 1981(Japan)
6) DIC174/DIC223
674 1) printing
2),3) Michio Ogura
4) Honmachi Print
5) 1976(Japan)
675 1) printing
3) Kazuharu Fujii
4) Handa Chuo Insatsu Co.,
Ltd.
5) 1981(Japan)

676 1) machine making
3) Kenji Kaneko
4) Hatsune Industry Co.,Ltd.
5) 1979(Japan)
677 1) television(sign)
3) Nikola Nikolov
4) Bulgarian T.V.
5) 1978(Bulgaria)
678 1) tourist agency
2) Iwao Miyanaga
3) Yasaburo Kuwayama
4) Hyakka Travel Center
5) 1977(Japan)
6) green/beige
679 1) construction
2),3) Guillermo Gonzalez Ruiz
4) Ianua
5) 1977(Buenos Aires)
6) red
680 1) gem dealer's shop
2) Harukata Yano
3) Hiro Terao
4) Gems Ishigami Nikko
5) 1982(Japan)
6) silver(DIC621)
681 1) medicine
2),3) Kazuo Tanaka
4) Torii & Co.,Ltd.
5) 1978(Japan)
6) DIC572/DIC220/DIC636
682 1) automobile
2),3) The design department
of the Isuzu Automobile
5) (Japan)
6) Isuzu red
683 1) steel
3) Damien Harrington
4) Irish Steel Limited
5) 1978(Ireland)
6) blue
684 1) bill
2) Thomas Ohmer
3) Carl Seltzer
4) The Income Fund of
America
5) 1973(Los Angeles)
6) brown
685 1) design studio
2),3) Gale W.Ikola
4) Ikola Designs
5) 1979(U.S.A.)
6) blue
686
2) Henry Steiner
3) Henry Steiner/Jennings Ku
4) The 'I' Club
5) 1982(Hong Kong)
6) black/white
687 1) interior
2),3) Shinsaku Mizuno
4) Ishimaru Interiors, Inc.
5) 1981(Japan)
688 1) planning
2),3) Norio Ikeda
4) Ikedamura Aseduction
5) 1980(Japan)
6) green
689 1) contracting
business(construction)
2),3) Angelo Sganzerla
4) Interchoice Contracting,
London
5) 1975(Milano)
690 1) electronic industry
2),3) Felix Beltran

4) Industria Electronica
5) 1976(Mexico)
6) gray
691 1) construction
2) Francisco Rendiles Coll
3) Armando Ferraro Senior
4) Interinca
5) 1978(Venezuela)
692 1) leasing
service(construction machinery)
2),3) Masami Taki
4) Idle Lease
5) 1979(Japan)
693 1) stockbroker
2),3) Fernando Rión
4) Inver México
5) 1980(Mexico)
6) green
694 1) papermaking
2),3) Madeleine Bujatti
4) Leykam
5) 1981(Austria)
6) black/blue
695 1) entertainment(trade
fair)
3) Sergio Salaroli/Michele
Spera
4) Internazionale Marmo
Machine
5) 1980(Rome)
6) black/white/orange
696
3) Duijvekshoff Daphne
4) Intomart Qualitatief
5) 1980(Holland)
6) black
697 1) culture centre
2),3) Paul Ibou
4) ICC-International Cult.
Centrum(Antwerp)
5) 1976(Belgium)
698 1) finance
2),3) Giovanni Brunazzi
4) IFI
5) 1976(Italy)
699 1) society(petroleum)
2),3) George McGinnis
4) Institute of French
Petroleum
5) 1982(New York)
700 1) research institute(golf)
2),3) Hiroshi Fukushima
4) IGR(International Golf
Research Institute)
5) 1983(Japan)
6) black/red(DIC159)
701 1) design studio
2),3) Arthur Eckstein
4) Typographic Images , Inc.
5) 1978(New York)
6) blue(PMS275)
702 1) bank
2),3) Chermayeff & Geismar
Associates
4) Illinois National Bank
5) (U.S.A.)
6) black/white
703 1) society(industry)
2),3) Tomás Vellvé
4) Instituto Nacional Industria
5) 1979(Barcelona)
6) black
704 1) society(orthopedics)
2),3) Walter Hergenröther
4) IOR Instituto Orthopedico

Rizzoli
5) 1971(Italy)
6) red
705 1) food(producing)
2),3) Francesco Burcini
4) IPM
5) 1982(Italy)
6) green/light green
706 1) petroleum
2),3) Silvio Coppola
4) Industria Pertolifera Sacca
5) 1972(Milano)
707 1) government agency(of
commerce)
2),3) Milton Glaser
4) New York State Dept.of
Commerce
5) 1975(New York)
6) black/red
708 1) fund
2),3) Paul Ibou
4) Interecho-uitgeversgroep
5) 1982(Belgium)
709 1) metalworking industry
2),3) Ivan Dvoršak
4) Impol,Slovenske Bistrica and
Dos Ljubljana
5) 1975(Yugoslavia)
6) silver
710 1) forestry
2),3) Gustavo Gomez
-Casallas/Rodrigo Fernandez
4) Industrial de Maderas
5) 1982(Colombia)
6) light yellow
711 1) trading concern
2) Félix Beltrán
3) Mónica Reyes
4) Interexport S.A.
5) 1983(Mexico)
6) brown
712 1) resort(camping
information)
3) István Szekeres
4) Kempinform
5) 1983(Budapest)
6) blue
713 1) manufactured
good(household goods)
2),3) Kanju Morohoshi
4) Imai Seisakusho Co.,Ltd.
5) 1981(Japan)
714 1) advertising agency
2),3) Tadamasa Katsube
4) Ichiko
5) 1983(Japan)
715 1) food
producing(confectionery)
2) The Commodity
Development Room of Ito
Seika
3) Yoshihiro Kishimoto
4) Ito Seika
5) 1979(Japan)
716 1) photograph(studio)
2),3) Shigeo Katsuoka
4) Ishihara Studio
5) 1981(Japan)
717
2),3) Jack Evens
4) Inter-Services
5) (U.S.A.)
718 1) information
2),3) Manfred Korten
4) HP.Bank

5) 1979(West Germany)
6) turquoise blue/black
719 1) research institute
3) Frutiger Adrian
4) Institut Atlantique
5) 1980(France)
720 1) manufactured
good(industry)
2),3) Robert L.Neumann
4) Imperial Clevite
5) 1980(U.S.A.)
6) blue
721 1) steel
2),3) Selahattin Sönmez
4) Iskenderun Demir Selik Steel
& Iron
5) 1976(Istanbul)
6) dark blue
722 1) investigation
2),3) Gustavo Gomez
-Casallas/Rodrigo Fernandez
4) Investigacines Para El
Desarrollo
5) 1983(Colombia)
6) red/blue
723 1) real property
2),3) Rinaldo Cutini
4) Immobiliare Erba
5) 1973/74(Rome)
6) brown
724 1) interior(carpets)
2),3) Selahattin Sönmez
4) Istanbul Carpet Centre
5) 1981(Istanbul)
6) ocher yellow
725 1) packing
2),3) Morfos Diseño
4) Impresos Kölonia
5) 1983(Mexico)
6) gray
726 1) wrapping,packing
2),3) Ivan Dvoršak
4) Ivica Lovinčič
5) 1978(Yugoslavia)
6) blue
727
2),3) Jürgen Spohn
4) Ingbau Berlin
5) 1974(West Berlin)
728 1) shipping line
2),3) Harry Murphy
4) United International
5) 1971(U.S.A.)
6) black/white
729 1) music(group)
2),3) Othmar Motter
4) Johann Strauss Orchestra
5) 1981(Austria)
6) black/white
730 1) construction
2),3) Fernando Rión
4) Constructora Jamsa
5) 1974(Mexico)
6) orange
731 1) clothing
2),3) Ikuya Kimura
4) Jupon Co.,Ltd.
5) (Japan)
732 1) electronics
2),3) Francesco Burcini
4) Jinotron
5) 1983(Italy)
6) light green/black
733 1) printing
3) Hermann Zapf

4) G.Jantsch's Printing Office
5) 1980(West Germany)
734 1) gem dealer's shop
2),3) Hideki Aoki
4) Jeweller Juko
5) 1982(Japan)
735
2) Debbie Mckinney
3) Mike Leidel
4) Chemjay Inc.
5) 1982(U.S.A.)
6) blue
736 1) private
symbol(designer)
2),3) Jagdish Chavda
4) J.J.Chavda
5) (U.S.A.)
737 1) technical art(joinery)
3) Kenneth Hollick
4) Greenwich Joinery, Limited
5) 1973(London)
6) green/white
738
2),3) Henry Steiner
4) Jardine Fleming & Co.,Ltd.
5) 1972(Hong Kong)
6) red
739 1) interior(furniture
making)
2),3) Mike Quon
4) Jeff Hirsch,Inc.
5) 1976(New York)
6) green
740 1) design studio
2),3) Richard Wittosch
4) Shiply/Jones Associates
5) 1979(U.S.A.)
6) black
741
2),3) Don Davis
4) Jeff O'Connor
5) 1976(U.S.A.)
6) red
742 1) travel ageney
2),3) Jacques N.Garamond
4) Jet-Tours
5) 1982(France)
6) black/blue
743 1) conference(economy)
2),3) Asher Kalderon
4) Jerusalem Economic
Conference
5) 1983(Israel)
6) silver
744 1) entertainment(fashion)
3) Ikko Tanaka
4) Japan External Trade
Organization
5) 1981(Japan)
745 1) private
symbol(designer)
2),3) Joe Dieter
4) Joe Dieter
5) 1971(U.S.A.)
6) black/relief
746 1) textile manufacture
2),3) Othmar Motter
4) J.M.Fussenegger
5) 1979(Austria)
6) black/white
747 1) food
2),3) Yoshihiro Kishimoto
4) Nippon Mineraru Kenkyujo
5) 1983(Japan)
748 1) food(producing)

Index to Contained Works

2) Akira Hirata
3) Akira Hirata／Koji Mori
4) Japan Riceland Co.,Ltd.
5) 1982(Japan)
749 1) textile good
2),3) Hidemi Nakazawa
4) Kanebo
5) 1983(Japan)
750 1) sport(group)
2) Akira Hirata
3) Akira Hirata／Koji Mori
4) Japan Golf Tournament Council
5) 1983(Japan)
751 1) farming
2),3) Bill Bundzak
4) Johanna Farm
5) 1976(New York)
6) red
752 1) private symbol
2),3) Joseph Churchward
4) Joseph Churchward
5) 1973(New Zealand)
753 1) international development organization
3) Sergio Salaroli
4) International Fund for Agriculture Development
5) 1976(Italy)
6) black
754 1) printing,educational apparatus(making,selling)
3) Shigeo Fukuda
4) Ideal Science Industry
5) 1979(Japan)
755 1) culture center
2),3) Othmar Motter
4) Culture Advancement Club Bregenz
5) 1982(Austria)
756 1) photo studio
2),3) Kazumasa Nagai
4) Kaburagi Studio
5) 1982(Japan)
757 1) investment trust
2),3) Herbert Wenn
4) Kicken Investment Firm
5) 1979(West Germany)
758 1) advertising agency
2) Claude-Marc Perrot
3) Jean-Claude Muller
4) Agence Ker
5) 1970(U.S.A.)
6) black
759 1) transportation
2),3) Ikuya Kimura
4) Kobe Shinkotsu Co.,Ltd.
5) 1979(Japan)
760 1) culture center
2),3) Sogen Onishi
4) Kansai Academy
5) 1983(Japan)
6) gray／pink
761 1) photo studio
2),3) Ken'ichi Hirose
4) Kobashi Photo Studio
5) 1974(Japan)
762 1) shop(fancy goods shop)
2),3) Koichi Watanabe
4) Kunimatsuya
5) 1979(Japan)
763 1) food(producing)
2) Akira Hirata
3) Akira Hirata／Koji Mori

4) OK Foods Co.,Ltd.
5) 1982(Japan)
764 1) real property
2) Gottschalk＋Ash International
3) Stuart Ash
4) Marathon Realty Co.,Ltd.
5) 1977(Toronto)
765 1) chamber of commerce and industry
2) Thomas Starr／Randall Swatek
3) Thomas Starr
4) Kailua Chamber of Commerce
5) 1973(U.S.A.)
6) blue／green／black
766 1) shop dealing in tool for Sunday carpentry
2),3) Nagato Kawamoto
4) Kanbun Co.,Ltd.
5) 1978(Japan)
767 1) commercial matter
2) Koichi Watanabe
3) Kunio Watanabe
4) Kutsuna Shoji Co.,Ltd.
5) 1974(Japan)
768 1) automobile(factory)
2),3) Sogen Onishi
4) Kuwahara Cars Co.,Ltd.
5) 1981(Japan)
769 1) distribution industry
2),3) Tsutomu Shimoyama
4) Kitazawa Distribution Industry
5) 1983(Japan)
770
2),3) Ed Penniman
4) Victor Kemp Company
5) 1980(U.S.A.)
6) PMS471／PMS409
771
2),3) Dawn Gustus
4) The Kuhne Co.(Champaign)
5) (U.S.A.)
6) black
772 1) furniture showroom
2),3) Harry Murphy
4) Kieffer Pacific
5) 1975(U.S.A.)
6) chrome foil
773 1) aluminium manufacture
2),3) Jack Evans
4) Krestmark
5) (U.S.A.)
774 1) restaurant
2),3) Chermayeff & Geismar Associates
4) The Krystal Company
5) (U.S.A.)
6) brown／red／yellow
775 1) private symbol(designer)
3) Chris Brand
4) Chris Brand
5) (Brussels)
776 1) trading company
2),3) Hiroshi Toida
4) Kaneda Enterprise, Inc.
5) 1983(Japan)
6) blue(VD 05c3)
777 1) textile
2),3) Akisato Ueda
4) Kanbe Co.,Ltd.

5) 1973(Japan)
778 1) investment and brokerage
3) Kenneth Hollick
4) Kellock Factors, Limited
5) 1976(London)
6) blue
779
2) Thomas Ohmer
3) Courtney Reeser
4) King Racing
5) 1980(Los Angeles)
6) gray
780 1) holding company
2),3) Selahattin Sönmez
4) Karaca Holding
5) 1978(Istanbul)
6) dark green
781 1) advertising agency
2),3) Joseph M.Bass
4) Kopel Ltd Adv.
5) 1970-83
782 1) photograph(film)
2) Joe Selame
3) Selame Design Group
4) Eastman Kodak Company
5) 1983(U.S.A.)
6) red／black／yellow
783 1) interior(wallpaper making)
2),3) Kazumasa Nagai
4) Kawakichi Co.,Ltd.
5) 1973(Japan)
784
2),3) Terry Lesniewicz／Al Navarre
4) Kennecorp
5) 1973(U.S.A.)
785 1) chain store
2) Kinya Zen
3) Takaaki Yoshinobu
4) Kahma Co.,Ltd.
5) 1981(Japan)
6) golden red(DIC117)
786 1) private symbol
3) Yoshikatsu Tami
4) Takahide Kurara
5) 1976(Japan)
787 1) foundation
2),3) Adam Moltke
4) Church Foundation
5) 1982(Denmark)
788 1) hospital
2),3) George Delany
4) Kent County Memorial Hospital
5) 1981(U.S.A.)
6) blue
789 1) plate making
2),3) Yukihisa Takakita
4) Kyowa Kosoku Seihan
5) 1978(Japan)
790 1) textile(clothes)
2),3) Stephan Kantscheff Raina Knjaginja Panaguriste
5) 1974(Bulgaria)
791 1) department store
2),3) Yasuhisa Iguchi
4) Kanayama
5) 1983(Japan)
792 1) society of shop owners
2),3) Shigeji Kobayashi
4) Kinshicho Shinkokai
5) 1979(Japan)
793 1) society(chemical shoe

making)
2),3) Jitsuo Hoashi
4) Japan Chemical Shoes Industries Association
5) 1983(New York)
6) black／red
794 1) planning
2),3) Sonja Wunderlich
4) Der Kinderbuchverlag Berlin
5) 1971(West Berlin)
795 1) food(producing)
2),3) Yoshihiro Yoshida
4) Kashiwa Shokuhin
5) 1981(Japan)
796 1) food(producing)
2) Teruo Ishikawa
3) Teruo Ishikawa／Mariko Kondo
4) Kawashin Sanshoku
5) 1982(Japan)
6) red
797 1) hotel
2),3) Osamu Ogawa
4) Kagaya
5) 1975(Japan)
798 1) molding technology
2),3) Harry Murphy
4) William Kreysler Association
5) 1982(U.S.A.)
6) blue／red
799 1) bookshop
2),3) István Szekeres
4) Könyvértékesitő Vállalat
5) 1978(Budapest)
800 1) information(television station)
3) Nikola Nikolov
4) Bulgarian T.V.
5) 1977(Bulgaria)
6) black／white
801 1) music(musical instrument manufacture)
2),3) Stefan Tchakarov
4) Kremona
5) 1976(Bulgaria)
6) black／white
802 1) private symbol(jazz critic)
3) Shigeo Yamaguchi
4) Kiyoshi Koyama
5) 1981(Japan)
803 1) design studio
2),3) Yukio Kanise
4) Kanise Design Jimusho
5) 1978(Japan)
804 1) design studio
2),3) Yasaburo Kuwayama
4) Kuwayama Design Room
5) 1982(Japan)
805 1) broker
2),3) James Lienhart
4) Kollar Heinz Inc.
5) (U.S.A.)
806 1) interior design
2) Mitsuo Ishida
3) Toshiro Abe
4) Ishida Research Institute of Construction
5) 1982(Japan)
807
2),3) Michael Baviera
4) Karl Künzle Switzerland
5) 1970(Zurich)
6) red
808 1) art museum

2) Lásió Pusvás
3) Ernö Sara
4) Képzömüvészeti Kiadó Art Publishing House
5) 1980(Budapest)
6) black
809 1) consultant (management)
2),3) Paul Ibou
4) KomKommer International
5) 1978(Belgium)
810 1) medicine
2),3) Scott Engen
4) K+K Medical USA
5) 1982(U.S.A.)
6) black/red(PMS032)
811 1) consultant (management)
2),3) Gavin Healy
4) Key Services Limited
5) 1970(London)
6) brown
812 1) advertising agency
2),3) Takaaki Yoshinobu
4) Orion Advertising Company
5) 1980(Japan)
813
3) Michael Herold
4) Anton koch
5) 1971(West Germany)
6) black/orange
814 1) printing
3) Sumio Hasegawa
4) Kato Insatsu
5) 1973(Japan)
815 1) jeweler(selling)
2) Katsuichi Ito
3) Katsumi Miyasaka
4) Kings Lay Co.,Ltd.
5) 1983(Japan)
6) gold
816 1) textile industry
2),3) Georg Staehelin
4) Klaus Soltau
5) 1977(Zürich)
6) dark blue
817 1) tourist agency
2),3) Stephan Kantscheff
4) Koopturist
5) 1970(Bulgaria)
818 1) planning
2),3) Akiyoshi Kuwahara
4) Toshi Kenchiku Kenkyusho
5) 1981(Japan)
819 1) advertising agency
3) Toshiaki Takahashi
4) Modern Advertisement
5) 1980(Japan)
820
2),3) Burton Kramer
4) Kypers,Adamson,Norton Ltd.
5) 1971(Toronto)
6) red
821 1) automobile(parts manufacture)
2) Sudarshan Dheer
3) Neelkamal Patil
4) Kalyani Brakes, Ltd.
5) 1983(India)
6) red/black
822 1) manufacturing good(thermometer)
2),3) Roberet Hargenhoffer
4) Kelvin Reserch Corporation

5) (U.S.A.)
823 1) systematic apparatus for the fish-luring light(making)
2),3) Masaaki Fukuda
4) Kitanippon Gyogyo Co.,Ltd.
5) 1983(Japan)
824 1) bank
2),3) Denise Spaulding
4) Kentucky Farmers Bank
5) 1980(U.S.A.)
6) brown
825 1) school
2),3) Takenobu Igarashi
4) Kanazawa Institute of Technology
5) 1983(Japan)
826
2),3) Stephan Kantscheff
4) Kurcrt Komplex
5) 1974(Bulgaria)
827 1) manufacturing goods(adhesive tape)
2),3) Claude Dieterich
4) Kuresa
5) 1980(Peru)
828 1) computer(selling)
2),3) Hisahiro Umezawa
4) Koyo Office Planning
5) 1983(Japan)
829 1) manufacturing good(plaything)
2),3) Warner Kopp
4) Kopptronix Co.
5) 1970(U.S.A.)
6) black
830 1) collectors' exchange
3) Michael Herold
4) Stuttgarter Messe-ound Kongress-GmbH
5) 1975(West Germany)
6) orange
831 1) office
3) Ikko Tanaka
4) Kitchen
5) 1978(Japan)
832 1) plastics industry
2),3) Othmar Motter
4) Kleiber
5) 1981(Austria)
833 1) music(group)
2),3) Kazuo Tajima
4) Kanagawa Philharmonic Orchestra
5) 1973(Japan)
6) black
834 1) city cultural promotion
2),3) Othmar Motter
4) Kulturkreis Hard
5) 1978(Austria)
6) black/white
835 1) construction
2) Hans Weber
3) Hansueli Maurer
4) Kurt Hungerbuhler
5) 1976(Zürich)
6) black
836 1) bank
2),3) Othmar Motter
4) Kantonalbank Appenzell
5) 1982(Austria)
837 1) culture center
2),3) Othmar Motter
4) Kulturzentrum Dornbirn
5) 1977(Austria)

838 1) private symbol(construction planner)
2),3) Yasaburo Kuwayama
4) Yashiro Kuwayama
5) 1978(Japan)
6) black/blue
839 1) interior(furniture making)
2),3) Stephan Kantscheff
4) Komsomolgz
5) 1972(Bulgaria)
840 1) bookshop
2),3) Fernando Medina
4) Liber '83
5) 1983(Madrid)
6) green
841 1) boutique
2),3) Giovanni Brunazzi
4) Labor Abbiguamento
5) 1972(Italy)
842
2),3) Hans E.Scheur
4) Photo+Litho Anstalt Weiss
5) 1973(West Germany)
6) red
843 1) silverware shop
2),3) Alfredo de Santis
4) Lembo
5) 1982(Rome)
844 1) paint(making)
2),3) Walter Hergenröther
4) Longo
5) 1970(Italy)
845 1) consultant (management)
2) Akira Hirata
3) Akira Hirata/Koji Mori/ Namiko Nishida
4) Nihon LCA Co.,Ltd.
5) 1983(Japan)
6) green(Pantone354)
846 1) steel manufacturing
2),3) Francesco Burcini
4) Linguaglossa
5) 1976(Italy)
6) blue
847 1) piano shop
2),3) Eita Shinohara
5) 1982(Japan)
848 1) medicine
2),3) Kazuo Tanaka
4) Torii & Co.,Ltd.
5) 1975(Japan)
6) DIC222,DIC122/DIC222, DIC91
849 1) sport(tennis club)
2),3) Teruo Fujishige
4) Ravuron Tennis Club
5) 1975(Japan)
850
2) Stankowski/Duschek
3) Anton Stankowski
4) RKW 9th Small Business Seminar
5) 1980(West Germany)
851 1) art exhibition
3) Paul Ibou
4) Linea
5) 1983(Belgium)
6) blue/green/red
852 1) sport(athletic club)
2) Haruo Akiyama
3) Kazuo Kanai
4) Beauty Athletic Inn Lady's
5) 1982

853 1) gallery
3) Rosmarie Tissi
4) Galerie Lopez
5) 1976(Switzerland)
6) green
854 1) engineering
2) Go Okazawa
3) Makoto Yoshida
4) Life Engineering Corporation
5) 1973(Japan)
6) blue(Pantone300)
855
2),3) Lanny Sommese
4) Ralph Licastro
5) 1979(U.S.A.)
6) blue/white
856 1) textile(textile industry)
2),3) Alfonso Capetillo Ponce
4) Lartel
5) 1979(Mexico)
6) blue
857 1) research institute(light)
2),3) Ettore Vitale
4) Instituto Luce
5) 1972(Rome)
858 1) printing(typesetting)
2),3) Felix Beltran
4) Letra y Linea
5) 1982(Mexico)
6) black
859 1) beauty salon
2),3) Koichi Watanabe
4) Beauty Salon:Lake
860 1) food(producing)
2),3) Silvio Gayton
4) Liquid Food,Inc.
5) 1981(U.S.A.)
6) black/gold
861 1) cleaning
2) Fernando Rión
3) Frank Carr/Fernando Rión
4) Linoblanc
5) 1981(Mexico)
6) dark blue/light blue
862
2),3) Fernando Medina
4) Lucentum
5) 1979(Madrid)
6) red
863
2),3) Claude Dieterich
4) Lavindustrias
5) 1977(Peru)
864 1) art store
2),3) Ed Penniman
4) Lenz Art Store
5) 1975(U.S.A.)
6) PMS185
865 1) photograph (producing)
2) Mike Quon/Steve Lim
3) Mike Quon
4) Steve Lim Productions
5) red/gray
866
2),3) Gavin Healey
4) The Lesser Group
5) 1971(London)
867
2),3) Silvio Coppola
4) Arpa
5) 1972(Italy)
868 1) bank
2) Thomas Ohmer

Index to Contained Works

3) Lou Frimkess
4) First Los Angeles Bank
5) 1975(Los Angeles)
6) green/blue
869 1) synthetic leather product
2) Yasunori Suzumori
3) Shigo Yamaguchi
4) Asahi Kasei
5) 1983(Japan)
870
2),3) Silvio Coppola
4) Leonblu
5) 1971(Italy)
871 1) sport(flying centre)
3) Matjaž Bertonceli
4) Flying Centre of Maribor
5) 1973(Yugoslavia)
6) blue
872
2),3) Oanh Pham-Phu
4) Ledebur Fliesen
5) 1970(Müchen)
6) black
873
3) Michael Herold
4) Lutz Feufel
5) 1970(West Germany)
6) blue
874 1) construction
2),3) Mike Quon
4) Lim Hirsch Inc.
5) 1977(New York)
6) blue
875 1) savings and loan
2),3) Rey Da Costa
4) La Industrial E.A.P.
5) 1972(Venezuela)
6) blue
876
2),3) Keith Murgatroyd
4) McLean Ltd.
5) 1981(London)
6) orange
877 1) publishing
2),3) Lanny Sommese
4) Leisure Press
5) 1975(U.S.A.)
6) blue/white
878
2),3) Hans Kündig
4) Lennart Larsson Rörled
5) 1981(Sweden)
6) black/red
879 1) restraurant
2),3) Fernando Rión
4) Los Rincones de Bosques
5) 1980(Mexico)
6) green(Pantone361)
880 1) printing
2),3) Morfos Diseño
4) Lito Sol
5) 1983(Mexico)
6) orange/yellow
881 1) transportation
3) Paul Ibou
4) Lagotainer
5) 1973(Belgium)
882 1) research institute(life and culture)
2),3) Fumio Koyoda
4) Life and Culture Research Institute
5) 1979(Japan)
883 1) institute

2),3) Jost Hochuli
4) Institute for Latin-American Studies at the University of St. Gallen
5) 1981(Switzerland)
6) black
884 1) public relations company
2),3) Mike Quon
4) Lloyd Chester Associated
5) 1972(New York)
6) brown/tan/red
885 1) electrical machinery(selling)
2) FHK Henrion
3) Team
4) London Electricity Board
5) 1973(London)
6) orange
886
3) Michael Herold
4) Landesstelle Für Betriebsschutz
5) 1977(West Germany)
6) blue
887 1) tourist bureau
2),3) Yasaburo Kuwayama
4) Leisure Information Center
5) 1979(Japan)
6) red
888 1) clothing
2) Shunji Ninomi
3) Tetsuharu Mabuchi
4) Lila
5) 1983(Japan)
889 1) tourist agency
2),3) Alfredo de Santis
4) Livenza Viaggi
5) 1981(Rome)
890 1) book(sale on commission)
2),3) Sonja Wunderlich
4) Leipziger Kommissions-und Buchhandel
5) 1971(Germany)
6) black
891 1) aviation
2),3) Asher Kalderon
4) Arikia Air Lines
5) 1971(Israel)
6) black/white
892 1) textile industry
3) Carlo Malerba
4) Leasint Spa
5) 1978(Italy)
893 1) picture gallery
2),3) Hugo Arape
4) Galeria Minotauro
5) 1978(France)
894 1) display
2),3) Ken'ichi Hirose
4) Murayama Inc.
5) 1982(Japan)
6) blue/green
895 1) information(television)
2),3) George McGinnis
4) Christian Broadcasting Network
5) 1982(New York)
896 1) movie
2),3) Alfredo de Santis
4) Milano Cinema
5) 1977(Rome)
897 1) plastics industry
2),3) Damien Harrington

4) Martello Plastics Ltd.
5) 1982(Ireland)
6) red
898 1) administrative organ
2),3) Tadahiko Ogawa
4) Gifu-Ken Kaji-Gun Mitake-cho
5) 1975(Japan)
899 1) chinaware(selling)
3) Kazuharu Fujii
4) Marufuku Co.,Ltd.
5) 1979(Japan)
900 1) sport
2),3) Stephan Kantscheff
4) Malina
5) 1972(Bulgaria)
901
2) Armando Milani/Maurizio Milani
3) Maurizio Milani
4) Magis Farmaceutici
5) 1974(Milano)
902 1) restaurant
2) Mitsuo Ishida
3) Tamami Sato
4) DH Foods
5) 1974(Japan)
6) golden red
903 1) air conditioning arrangement
2),3) Makoto Yoshida
4) Miyoshigasu CH Co.,Ltd.
5) 1973(Japan)
6) Pantone process blue
904
2),3) Don Davis
4) Meson Nuclear
5) 1976(U.S.A.)
6) black
905 1) computer
2),3) Minoru Takahashi
4) Medical Information Network Service
5) 1980(Japan)
906
2),3) Julien Van Der Wal
4) Millet(Sacs de Montagne)
5) 1975(Geneva)
6) blue/black/red
907 1) hotel
2),3) Satoshi Hatakeyama
4) Mizusawa Grand Hotel
5) 1981(Japan)
908 1) art museum
2),3) István Szekeres
4) Makói József A.Museum
5) 1981(Budapest)
909 1) medical appliance(selling)
2),3) Ken'ichi Hirose
4) Mental Health
5) 1979(Japan)
6) red
910 1) school
2),3) Robert Hargenhoffer
4) Middlesex County College
5) 1977(U.S.A.)
911 1) cloth(manufacturing)
2),3) Akisato Ueda
4) Matsubara Shirts
5) 1975(Japan)
912 1) electrical machinery
2),3) John S.Brown
4) Milebar Electronics
5) 1972(Canada)

6) blue
913 1) computer
2),3) Velizar Petrov
4) Ministry of Metallurgy -Computing Center
5) 1977(Bulgaria)
6) orange/dark blue
914 1) publishing
2),3) Helmut Salden
4) Malmberg Publishers
915 1) molds factory
2),3) Fernando Rión
4) Molds Industriales
5) 1982(Mexico)
6) red
916
2) Armando Milani/Maurizio Milani
4) Merope Spa Carte in Rotoli
5) 1976(Milano)
917 1) bank
2),3) Asher Kalderon
4) United Mizrachi Bank
5) 1978(Israel)
6) gold/brown
918 1) publishing
2),3) Don Connelly
4) Metrocraft Publishing
5) 1977(U.S.A.)
6) black
919 1) cloth(manufacturing)
2),3) Paul Ibou
4) Mesy Shirts
5) 1974(Belgium)
920
2) Debbie Mckinney
3) Kathie Plati
4) 1983(U.S.A.)
5) black
921 1) home supply
2) Iwao Miyanaga
3) Yasaburo Kuwayama
4) Mitsui Home
5) 1974(Japan)
6) red
922 1) cleaning and taking charge of buildings
2),3) Yasaburo Kuwayama
4) Maruko Birumen
5) 1977(Japan)
6) light blue
923 1) society
2) Gun Larson
3) Gun Larson/Kerstin Larson
4) Malmo Exhibition Certre
5) 1980(Sweden)
6) red(PMS172)
924 1) clothing store
2),3) Kazuo Ono
4) Modan
5) 1973(Japan)
925 1) transportation
2),3) Don Connelly
4) Modular Movers
5) 1972(U.S.A.)
6) black
926 1) industry group
2),3) Paul Ibou
4) Medithek
5) 1983(Belgium)
927 1) food industry
2) Shakespear Design Studio
3) Paul and Ronald Shakespear
4) Molinos Rio de la Plata Food Manufacturers

5) 1980(Buenos Aires)
6) green
928 1) real property
2) John Follis
3) Wayne Hunt
4) Mountaingate
5) 1975(U.S.A.)
6) brown
929 1) trade
2),3) Koichi Watanabe
4) Marukai Corporation
5) 1981(Japan)
930 1) society(management)
2),3) Joseph Boggs
4) Market Technicians
Association
5) 1980(U.S.A.)
6) red(PMS185)
931 1) mining industry
2) Mario Zamparelli
3) Jean-Claude Müller
4) Summa Corporation, Mining
Division
5) 1973(U.S.A.)
6) blue(PMS280)
932 1) mineral spring
2),3) Manfred Wutke
4) Nawinta, Bad Windsheim
Mineral Springs
5) 1979(West Germany)
6) red
933 1) publishing and
telecommunication
2),3) Scott Engen
4) Media Services, University of
Utah
5) 1983(U.S.A.)
6) black/red(PMS032)
934 1) textile(underclothes
manufacturer)
2),3) Francesco Burcini
4) Marcella
5) 1982(Italy)
6) black/red/blue
935 1) planning
2),3) Akisato Ueda
4) Matui Architectural Office
5) 1977(Japan)
936
2),3) Angelo Sganzerla
4) Multhipla, Milano
5) 1973(Italy)
6) black
937 1) interior
2),3) Félix Beltrán
4) Ministerio de la Industria
Ligera
5) 1980(Cuba)
6) ocher
938 1) art museum
2),3) Gerd Leufert
4) Museo "Jesus Soto"
5) 1970(Venezuela)
6) black
939 1) bookshop
2),3) Yasaburo Kuwayama
4) Bookshop Meibundo
5) 1973(Japan)
940 1) petroleum
2) Joe Selame
3) Selame Design Group
4) Mutual Oil Co.
5) 1972(U.S.A.)
6) red/orange
941 1) beauty salon

2) Osamu Ogawa
3) Yuji Kawachi
4) Masumi
5) 1975(Japan)
942 1) music(group)
2),3) Stephan Kantscheff
4) Marek
5) 1981(Bulgaria)
943 1) publishing
2),3) Stephan Kantscheff
4) Septemvri
5) 1975(Bulgaria)
944 1) picture gallery
2),3) Shigeo Katsuoka
4) Tohoku Kogyo Co./
Memorial Gallery
5) 1982(Japan)
6) dark blue(DIC222)
945 1) government agency
2) Gottschalk Ash International
3) Stuart Ash
4) Metric Commission
Government of Canada
5) 1973(Toronto)
6) red
946 1) art museum
2),3) Velizar Petrov
4) Museum "Kalaidjiisky"
5) 1982(Bulgaria)
6) red
947 1) building
material(manufacturing)
2),3) Sudarshan Dheer
4) Mahavir Refractories Pvt.,
Ltd.
5) 1973(Bombay)
6) brown
948 1) beverage
2),3) Hiroyuki Okuda
4) Hiei Kosen
5) 1981(Japan)
949 1) public undertaking
2),3) Kenneth Larsen
4) MMSD
5) 1977(U.S.A.)
6) blue
950 1) coating
2),3) Yasaburo Kuwayama
4) Maebara Coating
5) 1983(Japan)
6) green
951 1) real property
2),3) Terry Lesniewicz/Al
Navarre
4) Mohon Realty
5) 1974(U.S.A.)
952 1) office
equipment(manufacturing)
2),3) Francesco Burcini
4) Meccanografica
5) 1971(Italy)
6) black
953 1) picture gallery
2),3) Eita Shinohara
4) Gallery-Megu
5) 1978(Japan)
954 1) sample fair
2),3) Dieter Urban
4) Messe München
International
5) 1983(West Germany)
6) blue/black
955 1) textile
industry(knitwear)
2),3) Stepahn Kantscheff

4) Marek Kjustendil
5) 1982(Bulgaria)
956 1) research
institute(medium)
2),3) Michael Richards
4) Media Services University of
Utah
5) 1976(U.S.A.)
6) blue/green
957 1) sport(tournament)
2),3) Don Connelly
4) Metro Amateur Golf
Tournament
5) 1983(U.S.A.)
6) green
958 1) market
2),3) Gustavo Gomez
-Casallas/Rodrigo Fernandez
4) Mercadeo-Andigraf
5) 1983(Columbia)
6) black
959 1) construction
2),3) Ray Engle
4) Moffitt & McDaniel
Architects
5) 1970(U.S.A.)
6) blue/black
960 1) school
2),3) Gustavo Gomez
-Casallas/Rodrigo Fernandez
4) Golegio Maria Auxiliadora
5) 1978(Colombia)
6) light blue
961 1) private
symbol(sightseeing guide)
3) Yutaka Sato
4) Munuel Albo
5) 1979(Japan)
962 1) accessories shop
2),3) Eita Shinohara
4) Atelier MEGU
5) 1978(Japan)
963 1) industry
2),3) Sttephan Kantscheff
4) Milan Wasilev
5) 1972(Bulgaria)
964 1) insurance
2),3) Stan Brod
4) Malcolm Bernstein Insurance
Co.
5) 1983(U.S.A.)
965
2),3) Paul Ibou
4) Machines Collette(Nutrition
Machine)
5) 1974(Belgium)
966
2),3) Velizar Petrov
4) Ministry of Transport
-Computing Certre
5) 1979(Bulgaria)
6) red/black
967 1) metro savings and
loan
2) Cliff Chandler
3) Melanie Bass
4) Metro Savings & Loan
5) 1983(U.S.A.)
968 1) medical
appliance(manufacturing)
2),3) Paul Ibou
4) Medico Electronic
5) 1977(Belgium)
969 1) machine industry
2),3) Shunji Ninomi

4) Miyanami Engineering Co.,
Ltd.
5) 1980(Japan)
970 1) real property
2) Duane Wiens
3) Arvid Wallen
4) Matthews Real Estate
Company
5) 1979(U.S.A.)
6) blue
971 1) advertising agency
2),3) Scott Engen
4) Marcus Grant Advertising
5) 1982(U.S.A.)
6) black/blue
972 1) investment company
2),3) Robert Hargenhoffer
5) (U.S.A.)
973 1) hotel
2),3) Kao Yu-Lin
4) Taipei Miramar Hotel
5) 1979(Taipei)
6) brown
974 1) hat(making)
2) Yonefusa Yamada
3) Shin Sasaki
4) Maruishi
5) 1980(Japan)
975 1) office machine(selling)
2),3) Rinaldo Cutini
4) Marcello Masi
5) 1973(Rome)
6) black
976 1) metalworking industry
2),3) Jorge Sposari
4) Productos Metalicos
5) 1980(Mexico)
977 1) construction
2),3) Lanny Sommese
4) Michael Novak Construction
Company
5) 1975(U.S.A.)
6) blue/white
978 1) exhibition of metals
2),3) Michael Herold
4) Stuttgarter Messe-und
Kongress-GmpH
5) 1977(West Germany)
6) dark blue
979
3) Paul Ibou
4) Marc Wouters(Fototgraaf)
5) 1982(Belgium)
980 1) conference
2),3) Werner Schneider
4) Meeting 71
5) 1971(West Germanuy)
6) orange
981
2),3) Asher Kalderon
4) M.Rotenberg Industrial
Design
5) 1983(Israel)
6) black/orcher/yellow/
brown
982 1) museum
3) Frutiger Adrian
4) Musées Nationeaux de
France
5) 1974(France)
6) black
983 1) industry
2),3) Stephan Kantscheff
4) Prezis-Michai
5) 1972(Bulgaria)

Index to Contained Works

984 1) sample fair
2),3) Dieter Urban
4) Messe München
International
5) 1983(West Germany)
6) blue／black
985 1) transportation
2),3) István Szekeres
4) Anyagmozgatási Cs.
5) 1981(Budapest)
6) blue
986 1) beauty salon
2),3) Toshinori Nozaki
4) Beauty Salon Miyata
5) 1978(Japan)
987 1) security
2) Elias,Santamarina
3) Lose Santamarina
4) Mardin
5) 1971(Spain)
988 1) service(picture gallery)
2),3) Shigeo Katsuoka
4) Miwa Gallery
5) 1982(Japan)
6) light green(DIC92)
989 1) information(television station)
2),3) Eita Shinohara
4) Miyazaki Hoso
5) 1975(Japan)
990 1) loan servcice
2) Shizuo Yoneda
3) Koichi Watanabe
4) Marumiya
5) 1982(Japan)
991 1) landscape gardening
2),3) Yasuhisa Iguchi
4) Mitake Yogyo
5) 1983(Japan)
992 1) cosmetic(soap)
2),3) Fumio Koyoda
4) Max Co.,Ltd
5)1980(Japan)
993 1) automobile(servicing and selling)
2) Osamu Ogawa
3) Hajime Fujii
4) Mamekawa Jidosha
5) 1979(Japan)
994 1) cosmetic(soap,sets of towels)
2),3) Fumio Koyoda
4) Max Co.,Ltd.
5) 1980(Japan)
995 1) interior
2),3) Gustavo Gomez
-Casallas／Rodrigo Fernandez
4) Modul
5) 1983(Colombia)
6) red／black
996 1) museum
2),3) Felix Beltran
4) Museo Nacional
5) 1970(Mexico)
6) black
997 1) doll shop
2),3) Kazuho Tamamoto
4) Morishige Dolls
5) 1974(Japan)
6) golden red(Pantone032c)
998 1) wedding hall(general restaurant)
2),3) Shuji Torigoe
4) Nonaka Shokudo
5) 1973(Japan)
999 1) food(producing)

2) Jutaro Ito
3) Koichi Kanagawa
4) Maurzen
5) 1979(Japan)
6) red
1000 1) music school
2),3) Appelbaum＋Curtis
4) Manhattan School of Music
5) 1976(U.S.A.)
6) dark blue
1001 1) machine industry
2),3) Stephan Kantscheff
4) Textile Machine
5) 1980(Bulgaria)
1002 1) printing
3) Toshio Sonohara
4) Eishin Sha Co.,Ltd.
5) 1979(Japan)
1003
2),3) Michael Herold
5) 1976(West Germany)
6) red
1004 1) tourist agency
2),3) Oanh Pham-Phu
4) Maria Borucki
5) 1968(München)
6) blue
1005 1) culture center
2),3) Fumio Koyoda
4) Mainichi Culture Center
5) 1979(Japan)
1006 1) publicity company
2) Júlia Nemes
3) Erno Sára
4) Magyar Hirdeto／Hungarian
Publicity Company
5) 1978(Budapest)
6) dark blue
1007 1) publication
2),3) Shigeo Katsuoka
4) Sogensha Co.
5) 1983(Japan)
1008 1) school
3) A.G.Schillemans
4) Montessori School
5) 1974(Amsterdam)
6) orange
1009
2),3) Bob Swisher
4) Midwest Nuclear Inc.
5) (U.S.A.)
6) dark brown
1010 1) interior(furniture making)
3) G.Edwards
4) Mubles Norden
5) 1978(Mexico)
6) brown
1011
2) Armando Milani／Maurizio
Milani
3) Maruizio Milani
4) Mecort Meccanica pesante
5) 1979(Milano)
1012 1) printing
3) Kazuharu Fujii
4) Mizuno Print
5) 1976(Japan)
1013 1) building
material(concrete manufacture)
2),3) Bob Swisher
4) CBM Concrete Company
5) (U.S.A.)
6) orange
1014 1) design studio

2),3) Maria Mazzara
4) Design Group M
5) 1972(U.S.A.)
6) gray
1015 1) telecommunication
apparatus
2),3) Harumasa Misaki
4) Nichiei Tsushin Co.,Ltd.
5) 1983(Japan)
1016 1) decoration
material(manufacturing and
selling)
2),3) Tsuneyo Kamata／Kazuo
Tajima
4) Nakagawa Chemical
5) 1981(Japan)
6) blue
1017 1) sport(manufacturing
goods)
2),3) Kazuo Tajima
4) Nagase Rubber
5) 1979(Japan)
6) red／blue
1018 1) bank
2),3) Vasco Ceccon
4) National Bank of Canada
5) 1979(Montreal)
6) red
1019
2),3) Félix Beltrán
4) Deciep
5) 1972(Mexico)
6) black
1020 1) transportation
(container)
2),3) Koichi Watanabe
4) Nippon Unit Load Co.,Ltd.
5) 1977(Japan)
1021 1) real property
2),3) Shigeo Katsuoka
4) NAF Co.
5) 1980(Japan)
6) golden red(DIC159)
1022 1) planning
2),3) Shigeo Katsuoka
4) New Project Co.
5) 1980(Japan)
6) blue(DIC182)
1023 1) printing
2),3) Minoru Takahashi
4) Nikkei Printing,Inc.
5) 1982(Japan)
1024 1) patent office
2),3) Koichi Watanabe
4) Nakamura Patent Office
5) 1973(Japan)
1025 1) petroleum(products)
2) Kageyoshi Morishita
3) Kimio Oike
4) Nippon Oil
5) 1975(Japan)
1026 1) public undertaking
2),3) Gale W.Ikola
4) Northern States Power
5) 1977(U.S.A.)
6) green／blue
1027
2) Arnold Saks
3) Karl Hartig
4) Transnitro
5) 1972(New York)
6) green
1028 1) sport(goods)
2) Toru Sakuma
3) Toru Sakuma／Meiko Urata

4) Daiwa Sports Co.,Ltd.
5) 1982(Japan)
6) black(Pantone469c)／
red(Pantone485c)
1029 1) pottery manufacture
3) Kazuharu Fujii
4) Nishida Seisakusho
5) 1983(Japan)
1030 1) design studio
2),3) Tetsuo Noda
4) Noda Design Office
5) 1973(Japan)
1031 1) real property
2) Gottschalk＋Ash
International
3) Stuart Ash
4) Nocount Property
Development
5) 1974(Toronto)
1032 1) bookshop
2),3) Tetsuya Ota
4) Nankodo
5) 1980(Japan)
6) blue(ultramarine)
1033 1) printing
2),3) Rey R.Da Costa
4) Neografica
5) 1978(Venezuela)
6) brown
1034 1) museum(natural
science)
2),3) Jost Hochuli
4) Collection of Natural
Science of the Town of St.Gall
5) 1976(Switzerland)
6) black
1035 1) plastics industry
2) Fernando Rión
3) Jorge Carral／Fernando
Rión
4) Nacional de Resinas
5) 1978(Mexico)
6) blue／red
1036 1) construction(road
repairs)
2),3) Rolf Harder
4) Novaroad Ltd.
5) 1980(Montreal)
6) red
1037 1) leisure industry
2),3) Ken'ichi Kaneko
4) Nitto Kogyo Co.,Ltd.
5) 1977(Japan)
1038 1) men's wear shop
2),3) Robert P.Gersin
4) National Shirt Shops
5) 1979(New York)
6) various
1039 1) bank
2),3) João Carlos Cauduro／
Ludovico Antonio Martino
4) Banco Noroeste
5) 1973(São Paulo)
1040 1) music(office)
2),3) Yasumasa Oka
4) Nishimura Music House
5) 1972(Japan)
1041 1) transportation(marine
transportation)
2) Asher Kalderon
3) Asher Kalderon／T.Kleiner
4) Netra
5) 1971(Israel)
6) blue
1042 1) shopping center

2),3) Tetsuo Noda
4) Nichimo Shop Co.
5) 1973(Japan)
1043 1) food(producing)
2) Fernando Rión
3) Eduardo Zapata
4) Nutresa S.A.
5) 1981(Mexico)
6) orange(Pantone165c)
1044 1) hotel
2),3) Manfred Korten
4) Hotel Nassauer
5) 1972(West Germany)
6) dark blue
1045 1) real property
2),3) Katsuyoshi Yoshinaga
4) Nissen Kaihatsu
5) 1974(Japan)
1046 1) aviation
2),3) Steve Allen
4) National Aircraft
5) 1983(U.S.A.)
6) blue
1047 1) movie(producing)
2),3)Robert A. Gale
4) Nino Films Ltd.
5) 1976(New York)
6) black
1048
2) Ed Penniman
4) National Mortagage
5) 1982(U.S.A.)
6) PMS300/PMS185
1049 1) committee(taking
charge of a port)
2),3) Ove Engström
4) Norrkopings Hamn
5) 1975(Sweden)
6) light blue/dark blue
1050 1) society(league of
meat processors)
2),3) Hidemichi Yamao
4) League of Meat Processing
Minor Enterprisers
5) 1980(Japan)
1051 1) automobile
part(manufacturing and selling)
3) Yasaburo Kuwayama
4) Nippon Electric Apparatus
5) 1981(Japan)
6) red
1052 1) construction
2),3) Akiyoshi Kuwabara
4) Nihon Jutaku Maintenance
5) 1981(Japan)
1053 1) sport(team)
2),3) Philip Gips
4) New Rochelle Youth Soccer
Team
5) 1983(New York)
6) purple/yellow/white
1054 1) theatre
2) F.H.K. Henrion
3) F.H.K. Henrion/Jandenis
4) National Theatre
5) 1975(London)
6) black
1055 2) Michael J.Russell
3) Sylvia Sewell
4) New Product Management
Group
5) 1979(London)
6) red/white/blue
1056 1) municipal emblem
2) Robert P.Gersin

3) Robert P.Gersin/Johann
Schumacher
4) City of Niagara Falls
5) 1980(New York)
6) red/white/blue
1057
2),3) Los Shakespear
4) (Buenos Aires)
1058 1) sport(swimming club)
2),3) Gustavo Gomes
-Casallas/Rodrigo Fernandez
4) Club Neptuno
5) 1980(Colombia)
6) blue/yellow
1059 1) circulation
3) Yukio Koga
4) Nafuko
5) 1980(Japan)
6) blue(DIC182)
1060 1) real property
2),3) Ed Penniman
4) Noren-Aust Real Estate
5) 1978(U.S.A.)
6) PMS185
1061 1) circulation
2) Tadashi Ishikawa
3) Tadashi Ishikawa/Hideko
Sakato
4) Nakajima Hozando
5) 1980(Japan)
1062
2),3) Stephan Kantscheff
4) Powel Kortchagin
5) 1974(Bulgaria)
1063 1) snack bar
2),3) Tetsuo Noda
4) Fujita Shokai
5) 1975(Japan)
1064 1) sport(golf club)
2),3) Yasaburo Kuwayama
4) Narita Sunny Country Club
5) 1976(Japan)
6) blue/red
1065 1) laboratory(optic
nerve)
2) Tim Larsen
4) Optical Peripherals
Laboratory
5) 1982(U.S.A.)
6) black/rainbow
1066 1) landscape gardening
2),3) Shintaro Ajioka
4) Okamoto Takashi Landscape
Gardening Room
5) 1983(Japan)
1067 1) food(wholesale trade
and selling)
2) Shigeo Katsuoka
3) Shigeo Katsuoka/Hiroshi
Asami
4) Nihon Shurui Hanbai Co.
5) 1979/1981(Japan)
6) dark blue(DIC222)
1068 1) interior(furniture
making)
2) Shigeru Sato
3) Haruhiko Enomoto
4) Otsuka Kagu
5) 1980(Japan)
1069 1) transportation
2) Ove Engström
3) Ove Engström/Ingvar
Johansson
4) County Transport Company
5) 1982(Sweden)

6) black
1070 1) hospital(dentistry)
2),3) Koichi Watanabe
4) Ota Dental Clinic
5) 1974(Japan)
1071 1) society(health)
2),3) R.Roger Remington
4) Genesee Valley Group
Health Association
5) 1973(New York)
6) blue(Pantone300)
1072
2),3) Don Connelly
4) Organizational Services Inc.
5) 1977(U.S.A.)
6) gray
1073 1) beauty culture(goods)
2),3) Yoshihiro Yoshida
4) Beauty Clinic Ohara
5) 1980(Japan)
1074 1) exhibition
2),3) Stephan Kantscheff
4) Bulgarian Exhibition in
Okinawa
5) 1974(Bulgaria)
1075
2),3) Heinz Waibl
4) Centro Forme
5) 1975(Milano)
1076
2),3) Chermayeff & Geismar
Associates
4) Owens-Illinois
5) (U.S.A.)
6) blue/red
1077 1) society(recreation)
2),3) John S.Brown
4) Ontario Recreation Society
5) 1973(Canada)
6) green/ocher
1078
2),3) Rey R.Dacosta
4) Grupo Juridico OM
5) 1977(Venezuela)
6) green(olive)
1079 1) publishing(publication
on music)
2) Shin Nagamatsu
3) Kyoji Nakatani
4) ON Associates, Publisher of
Music Books
5) 1973(Japan)
1080 1) optical industry
2) Elias Santamarina
3) Jose Santamarina
4) Optica "Piñile"
5) 1981(Spain)
6) black
1081 1) transportation
2) Gottschalk+Ash
International
3) Sturart Ash
4) Oakville Transit
5) 1973(Canada)
1082 1) real property
2),3) F.R.Esteban
4) Oliver Tyrone Corporation
5) 1970(U.S.A.)
6) black
1083 1) paper and packaging
2),3) Rinaldo Cutini
4) Ondulato Umbro
5) 1974(Rome)
6) black
1084 1) trade(market)

2),3) Joseph M.Bass
4) Samet
5) 1970-1983
1085 1) guild(technical art)
2),3) Burton Kramer
4) Ontario Guild of Crafts
5) 1970(Toronto)
6) purple/ocher
1086 1) computer
2),3) Peter Wildbur
4) Overseas Computer
Consultants, Ltd.
6) green
1087 1) design studio
2),3) Takeshi Ohtaka
4) Ohtaka Design Production
5) 1975(Japan)
1088 1) government
agency(campaign)
2),3) Félix Beltrán
4) Departmento de Orientacion
Revolucionaria, Havana
5) 1973(Cuba)
6) brown
1089 1) funeral
2),3) Ron Richards
4) Ontario Funeral Services
Association
5) 1975(Toronto)
6) blue
1090 1) cooperative
association(ironware)
2),3) Ikuya Kimura
4) Ironware Dealers'
Cooperative Association of Ono
City
5) 1982(Japan)
6) red
1091
2),3) Arthur Eckstein
4) American Auto Federation
5) 1978(New York)
6) black
1092
2),3) Maurizio Milani/
Armando Milani
4) OSC Italia
5) 1979(Milano)
1093 1) computer(software
system)
2),3) Kenji Suzuki
4) Oriental System
Development, Inc.
5) 1983(Japan)
1094 1) music
3) Karol Śliwka
4) Polfrakt
5) 1982(Poland)
6) black
1095
2),3) R.Roger Remington
4) Panalogic Inc.
5) 1972(New York)
6) black/green(PMS369)
1096 1) leasing service(ships)
2) Katusmi Nagata/Yasaburo
Kuwayama
3) Yasaburo Kuwayama
4) Palace Shipping
5) 1973(Japan)
6) yellowish red
1097
2),3) Pietro Galli
4) Plasticone
5) 1975(Italy)

6) black
1098 1) mining
2),3) Felix Beltran
4) Pulvitec
5) 1982(Mexico)
6) black
1099 1) petroleum(refining)
2) Joe Vera
3) Francisco Tellez/Joe Vera
4) Petroquimicos y Polimeros
5) 1974(Mexico)
6) black
1100 1) construction planning
2),3) Shigeo Katsuoka
4) Panom Co.
5) 1980(Japan)
6) dark purple(DIC233)
1101 1) bank
2),3) James Lienhart
4) Pacesetter Bank
5) (Chicago)
1102 1) typesetting(electronic typesetting)
2),3) James Lienhart
4) Photoronic Typographers, Inc.
5) (Chicago)
1103 1) real estate development
2) Harry Murphy
3) Harry Murphy/Stanton Klose
4) Peter Paulsen
5) 1978(U.S.A.)
6) brown
1104 1) sounder (manufacturing)
2),3) Morfos Diseño
4) Grupo Pasec
5) 1982(Mexico)
6) dark purple
1105 1) printing
2) Edith Capan
3) Edith Capan/Bob Swisher
4) Printer Devil
5) (USA)
6) black/red
1106 1) construction
2),3) Joe Vera/Jose Luis Ortiz
4) Pyteco
5) 1972(Spain)
6) Ochre
1107 1) electric appliance(manufacturer)
2) Ove Engström
3) Ove Engström/Torgny Gustavsson
4) Petronic
5) 1979(Sweden)
6) light brown
1108 1) planning
2),3) Sadao Sugaya
4) Pitori Pikori
5) 1975(Japan)
6) red
1109
2) Wojciech Jaszczuk
3) Jan Hollender
4) Polonia
5) 1981(Poland)
6) black/white/red
1110 1) development
2),3) Rick Cartledge
4) Purdy's Wharg Development Limited

5) 1982(Canada)
6) PMS541
1111 1) petroleum
2),3) Fernando Rión/Eduardo Zapata
4) Petroleos Mexicanos
5) 1980(Mexico)
6) green/red
1112 1) hotel chain
2),3) Sudarshan Dheer
4) Poonam International Hotels
5) 1973(Bombay)
6) cobalt blue
1113 1) music(orchestra)
3) Szekeres István
4) Postás Szimfonikus
5) 1979(Hungary)
6) green
1114 1) employment agency
2),3) Ed Bohon
4) Placement Services
5) 1972(New York)
6) black
1115 1) security
2),3) Silvio Gayton
4) Protech Security Systems
5) 1983(U.S.A.)
6) azure blue
1116 1) taking in and discharging cargo
2),3) José Santamarina
4) Promusel
5) 1983(Spain)
6) black
1117
2),3) Ivan Dvoršak
4) Univerza Mariboru P.A.
5) 1980(Yugoslavia)
6) black
1118 1) entertainment
2),3) R.Roger Remington
4) Town of Penfield USA Bicentennial Committee
5) 1976(New York)
6) red/blue
1119 1) heavy machine
2),3) Jack Evans
4) Patterson
5) (U.S.A.)
1120 1) theatre
2),3) F.R.Esteban
4) Parable Players
5) 1983(U.S.A.)
6) black
1121
2),3) Jack Evans
4) Potomac Mortgage Company
5) (U.S.A.)
1122 1) bank
2),3) Ed Penniman
4) Pajaro Valley Bank
5) 1983(U.S.A.)
6) PMS469
1123 1) printing
2),3) Mo Lebowitz
4) Phoenix Typographers
5) 1982(New York)
6) black
1124 1) real estate
2),3) Jost Nochuli
4) Kurt Peyer
5) 1976(Switzerland)
6) black

1125
2),3) Hans Kündig
4) Tryggue System
5) 1982(Sweden)
6) green
1126 1) society(mountains)
2),3) Giovanni Burnazzi
4) Pila
5) 1979(Italy)
6) black/red
1127 1) plastics factory
2),3) Fernando Rión
4) Polimeros y Ameanto
5) 1982(Mexico)
1128 1) food producer(bread)
3) Judita Skalar
4) Pecivo
5) 1982(Yugoslavia)
6) brown
1129
2),3) Ricardo Rey
4) Papelera del Plata,Inc.
5) 1977(Puerto Rico)
6) red/black
1130 1) gem(selling)
2) Sudarshan Dheer
3) Neelkamal Patil
4) P.D.Kothari & Co.
5) 1982(India)
6) copper
1131
2),3) Steve Shelden
4) Peter James & Associates
5) 1977(U.S.A.)
6) dark gray
1132 1) construction
2),3) Elias Garcia Benavides
4) Promocinoes Pando
5) 1981(Spain)
6) red/indigo
1133 1) zoological garden
2),3) Jost Hochuli
4) Alpine Zoo
5) 1977(Switzerland)
6) black
1134 1) sport(manufacturing goods)
2),3) Rey R.Dacosta
4) Paseo
5) 1980(Venezuela)
6) dark brown
1135 1) recreation center
2),3) Stan Brod
4) Playhouse in the Park
5) 1970(U.S.A.)
6) dark green
1136 1) photograph(studio)
2),3) Tadamasa Katsube
4) Kumagai Shashinkan
5) 1978(Japan)
1137 1) hotel
2),3) Burton Kramer
4) Pinestone Inn
5) 1975(Toronto)
6) green
1138
2),3) Steve Shelden
4) P & S Services
5) 1983(U.S.A.)
6) green
1139 1) design studio
3) Kazuo Kanai
4) Planning One
5) 1979(Japan)
1140 1) real estate

2),3) Aluin Joe
4) Peninsula Brokers, Inc.
5) 1982(U.S.A.)
6) red/black
1141
2),3) Kip Reynolds
4) Pacific Data Images
5) 1983(U.S.A.)
6) blue/black
1142
2),3) Arthur Eckstein
4) P.I.E.Facilities,Inc.
5) 1971(New York)
6) black
1143 1) music(group)
2),3) Guillermo Gonzalez Ruiz
4) PMA
5) 1975(Buenos Aires)
6) red
1144 1) guild(metal work)
3) Jiři Rathousky
4) Napako
5) 1981(Czechoslovakia)
6) blue
1145 1) society(PTA)
2),3) Edward Hughes
4) The National Parent and Teachers Association
5) 1977(U.S.A.)
1146
2),3) Los Shakespear
5) (Argentina)
1147 1) fuel
2),3) Tatsuhito Yamamoto
4) Pacific Fuel Trading Co.
5) 1983(Japan)
6) yellow/blue
1148 1) education(program)
2),3) Dicken Castro
4) Tratamiento y Orientacion
5) 1975(Colombia)
1149 1) sport(club)
2),3) Giovanni Brunazzi
4) Gruppo Sportivo
5) 1974(Italy)
1150 1) jewelry(selling)
2),3) Giovanni Brunazzi
4) Polydiamants
5) 1971(Italy)
1151 1) interior(selling)
2),3) Giovanni Brunazzi
4) Paguano Arredamenti
5) 1970(Italy)
6) red
1152 1) restaurant(chain system)
2),3) Bruce D.Zahor/Joel Mitnick
4) Ponpizoo
5) 1982(New York)
6) blue/yellow
1153 1) information(sports program)
2) Mike Quon/Chris Zoulamis
3) Mike Quon
4) Paracom,Inc.
5) 1977(New York)
6) blue
1154 1) construction
2),3) Giovanni Brunazzi
4) Presspau
5) 1970(Italy)
6) red
1155 1) hotel
2),3) Ikuya Kimura

4) Kobe Portpia Hotel
5) 1980(Japan)
6) blue(DIC183)
1156 1) agriculture
2),3) Stephan Kantscheff
4) Sora
5) 1972(Bulgaria)
1157 1) food
2) John DiGianni
3) Gianninoto Associates,Inc.
4) Plumrose,USA
5) 1976(U.S.A.)
6) red/blue
1158 1) medicine
2),3) Kazuo Tanaka
4) Torii & Co.,Ltd.
5) 1977(Japan)
6) DIC222
1159 1) interior
2),3) Stephan Kantscheff
4) Rila
5) 1970(Bulgaria)
1160 1) chemical industry
2),3) Stephan Kantscheff
4) Rachovez
5) 1972(Bulgaria)
1161 1) construction
2) Keith Murgatroyd
3) Tony Forster
4) Varioplan
5) 1975(Manchester)
6) gray/black
1162 1) boutique
2),3) Yasaburo Kuwayama
4) Pan Mode
5) 1978(Japan)
6) black/purple
1163
2) Don Young
3) Don Young/Brian Lovell
4) Pacific Southwest Mortgage
5) 1982(U.S.A.)
1164 1) textile industry
2),3) Stephan Kantscheff
4) Rodina
5) 1982(Bulgaria)
1165 1) hospital
2),3) Edward Hughes
4) The Evanston Hospital
5) 1981(U.S.A.)
1166 1) entertainment
3) Jarostaw Jasinski
4) Centralne Dozynki w Plocku
5) 1976(Poland)
6) multicoloured
1167 1) publishing
2),3) Appelbaum+Curtis
4) Patient Care Products
5) 1978(New York)
1168 1) recreation center
2),3) João Carlos Cauduro/
Ludovico Antonio Martino
4) Playcenter
5) 1973(São Paulo)
1169 1) sounds
(manufacturing)
3) Paul Ibou
4) Photocompo Center
5) 1970(Belgium)
1170 1) art gallery
2) John Follis
3) James Potocki
4) People's Gallery
5) 1970(Los Angeles)
1171 1) precious metals

2),3) Ryuji Hirotani
4) Prime Jewelry
5) 1983(Japan)
1172
2),3) Dicken Castro
4) Projuventud
5) 1979(Colombia)
1173 1) interior
2),3) Stephan Kantscheff
4) Rodopi
5) 1982(Bulgaria)
1174 1) printing(campaign)
2),3) Hideki Aoki
4) Haneisha Printing
5) 1979(Japan)
1175 1) parking zone
2),3) Scott Engen
4) Parking Services
5) 1977(U.S.A.)
6) black/blue
1176 1) shoe shop
3) Paul Ibou
4) Piessens(shoemaker)
5) 1981(Belgium)
1177 1) interior
2),3) Stephan Kantscheff
4) Rodoposka Takan
5) 1976(Bulgaria)
1178 1) insurance
2),3) Ricardo Rey
4) Professional Group
Insurance
5) 1978(Puerto Rico)
6) gray/gold
1179 1) society(plumbing and
machine)
2),3) Dennis Pehoski
4) Plumbing and Mechanical
Contractors Association
5) 1981(U.S.A.)
6) blue/light gray
1180
2),3) Denise Spaulding
4) Quorum Corporation
5) 1983(U.S.A.)
6) orange
1181
3) Richard Eckersley
4) Donegal Quarttite, Limited
5) 1978(Ireland)
6) red
1182 1) development
2),3) Scott Engen
4) Quadrant,Inc.
5) 1981(U.S.A.)
6) black/blue
1183 1) textile industry
2),3) Rolf Harder
4) Queenswear,Inc.
5) 1973(Montreal)
6) black
1184 1) agriculture
2) R.Nava/D.Soffientini/A.
Ubertazzi/G.Romani
3) Da Centro Peril Disegno
Ambientale
4) Agriquality
5) 1980(Italy)
6) green
1185 1) design studio
2),3) Mike Quon
4) Mike Quon Design Office,
Inc.
5) 1970(New York)
6) gray

1186 1) private
symbol(pharmacist)
2),3) Mike Quon
4) Jeff Quon
5) 1982(New York)
6) red/blue
1187 1) printing(public
relations magazine)
2) Kuniharu Masubuchi
3) Hiroshi Iseya
4) Mikimoto Co.,Ltd.
5) 1981(Japan)
1188
2),3) Rick Cartledge
4) Quinpool Center
Developments Limited
5) 1977(Canada)
6) dark brown(PMS116)
1189 1) printing
2),3) Giancarlo Iliprandi
4) Honeywell Information
System
5) 1983(Milano)
6) black
1190 1) construction planning
2) Shigeo Katsuoka
3) Shigeo Katsuoka/Takahiro
Inoue
4) Q and Q Co.
5) 1976(Japan)
6) dark purple(DIC234)
1191 1) printing
2) Dave Hackett
3) Ken Eichenbaum
4) Quad Graphics
5) 1974(U.S.A.)
6) black/red/yellow/blue
1192
2),3) Philip Gips
4) Exxon Corporation
5) 1979(New York)
6) multicoloured
1193 1) entertainment
(international fashion design)
2),3) Jost Hochuli
4) Rencontre de Jeune Talent
5) 1982(Switzerland)
6) black
1194 1) papermaking
2),3) Burton Kramer
4) Reed Paper, Ltd.
5) 1974(Toronto)
6) orange
1195 1) insurance
2),3) Oanh Pham-Phu
4) Ravenburger Versicherung
5) 1980(München)
6) bluish gray
1196 1) bank
3) Yasaburo
Kuwayama(supervisor)
4) Bank of the Ryukyus
5) 1979(Japan)
6) red
1197 1) art museum
3) Frutiger Adrian
4) Musée Rodin Paris
5) 1980(France)
6) black
1198
2),3) Diana Graham
4) Rothchild
5) 1979(New York)
6) green
1199 1) society(racquet ball

league)
2),3) Yukio Kanise
4) Nihon Racquetball Renmei
5) 1981(Japan)
6) red/blue
1200
2) Gottschalk+Ash
International
3) Peter Adam
4) Rug Tuffers,Inc.
5) 1976(Toronto)
1201
2),3) Pietro Galli
4) Redaelli-Como
5) 1978(Italy)
6) black
1202 1) pharmacy
2),3) Giancarlo Iliprandi
4) Ribbon
5) 1979(Milano)
6) red
1203 1) design studio
2),3) Armando Milani
4) Reflex Design
5) 1981(Milano)
1204 1) publishing
2) Ronald Cutro
3) Cutro Associates,Inc.
4) Ranno Book Publishers
5) 1975(U.S.A.)
6) blue
1205 1) sport(sports shop)
2),3) Masakazu Tanabe
4) Rakuzanso
5) 1983(Japan)
1206 1) machine industry
2),3) João Carlos Cauduro/
Ludovico Antonio Martino
4) Indústrias Romi
5) 1972(São Paulo)
1207
2),3) Armando Milani
4) Regent International
5) 1979(Milano)
1208 1) education
2) Ray Engle
3) Ken White
4) Pharmeasea Services
5) 1974(U.S.A.)
6) blue/green
1209 1) hospital(dentistry)
2),3) Yukio Kanise
4) Royal Dental Office
5) 1977(Japan)
1210 1) sport(swmming club)
2),3) Gustavo Gomez-Casallas
Rodrigo Fernandez
4) Recreacutica Club
5) 1976(Colombia)
6) light blue
1211 1) manufactured goods
2),3) Oanh Pham-Phu
4) Rothschild GmbH
5) 1980(München)
6) gold/silver/blue
1212 1) entertainment
2),3) Herbert Binneweg
4) Town of Antwerp
International Rubens Year
5) 1977(Belgium)
6) black
1213
2),3) Pat Taylor
4) Billrolle & Associates
5) 1978(U.S.A.)

6) black
1214 1) music(records)
3) Kazuo Kanai
4) Radio City Record
5) 1978(Japan)
6) golden red
1215 1) service(group)
3) Szekeres István
4) Rendezvény Iroda
5) 1981(Hungary)
1216 1) air conditioning
installation
2) John Follis
3) James Potocki
4) Republic Air Conditioning
5) 1973(Los Angeles)
6) blue
1217 1) construction(road)
2),3) Don Connelly
4) Reynolds Asphalt Paving
5) 1976(U.S.A.)
6) black
1218 1) auto repair shop
2),3) Fernando Rión
4) Reconsa
5) 1979(Mexico)
6) blue
1219 1) photograph
(competition)
2),3) Giovanni Brunazzi
4) Premio di Fotografia Ratti
5) 1971(Italy)
1220 1) design
2),3) Jack Evands
4) Reiser Associates
Commercial/Designer Carpets
5) (U.S.A.)
1221 1) consultant
2),3) Rick Cartledge
4) R.A.Consultants, Limited
5) 1982(Canada)
6) dark blue/light blue
1222 1) construction planning
office
2),3) Akisato Ueda
4) RA Research Laboratory of
Architectural Space
5) 1975(Japan)
1223 1) bank
2) Michael Leidel
3) Kathie Burgund
4) Rochester Community
Savings Bank
5) 1983(Atlanta)
1224 1) excavation company
2),3) Denise Spaulding
4) Robinson Excavating
5) 1980(U.S.A.)
6) green/brown
1225 1) printing
2),3) Kimito Ohashira
4) Kowa Art Printing
5) 1979(Japan)
1226 1) private symbol
2),3) Tony Forster
4) FE&K Richardson
5) 1977(Manchester)
6) blue
1227 1) lock and
key(manufacturing)
2) Gottschalk+Ash
International
3) Stuart Ash
4) Reilly Lock Corporation
5) 1972(Toronto)

1228 1) design studio
2) Keith Murgatroyd
3) Tony Forster
4) Royle Murgatroyd Design
Associates, Ltd.
5) 1980(Manchester)
6) light green
1229
2),3) Manfred Wutke
4) Rangau-Quelle
5) 1979(West Germany)
6) blue
1230 1) automobile
2),3) The design department
of the Isuzu Automobile
4) The Isuzu Automobile
Industry
5) 1980(Japan)
6) black/red/gold
1231 1) sport(goods)
2),3) John M,Alexander
4) R & R Custom Boats
5) 1977(U.S.A.)
6) black
1232 1) breeding ground of
studhorses
2),3) Guillermo Gonzalez Ruiz
4) Rincon Roxans
5) 1982(Buenos Aires)
6) brown
1233 1) energy conservation
2),3) Harry Murphy
4) The House Doctors
5) 1982(U.S.A.)
6) black/white
1234 1) private inquiry agency
2) R.Nava/G.Romani/D.
Soffientini/A.Ubertazzi
3) Da,Centro Peril Disegno
Ambientale
4) Ricerca Quadri
5) 1979(Italy)
6) green
1235 1) ironwork
2) Ray Engle
3) Jerome Jensik
4) Reliance Steel Company
5) 1971(Los Angeles)
6) blue/black
1236 1) construction
2),3) Oanh Pham-Phu
4) Ringbau
5) 1975(München)
6) reddish brown
1237 1) auto part sales
2),3) Rey R.Dacosta
4) Juan R.Dacosta
5) 1970(Venezuela)
6) blue
1238 1) investment company
2),3) Rey R.Dacosta
4) Rendiven
5) 1976(Venezuela)
6) brown
1239 1) publishing
2),3) Sudarshan Dheer
4) Ross Murarka(India)
5) 1971(Bombay)
6) black/red
1240 1) construction
2),3) Richard Wittosch
4) Redi-Mix Associates,Inc.
5) 1980(U.S.A.)
6) gray

1241
2),3) Madeleine Bujatti
4) Schiress
5) 1978(Austria)
6) dark blue/red
1242
2),3) Paul Ibou
4) Rubens Stevedoring
5) 1977(Belgium)
1243 1) tin work
2),3) Francesco Burcini
4) Solfer
5) 1978(Italy)
6) silver
1244 1) plastic Industry
2) R.Nava/D.Soffientini/A.
Ubertazzi
3) Environmental Design
Center
4) Sogiplast
5) 1982(Italy)
6) green
1245 1) haberdasher's store
2) Akira Hirata
3) Akira Hirata/Hiroshi Tada
4) Petit Maison Shimazaki
5) 1977(Japan)
6) Pantone294c
1246 1) trade
2),3) Ikuya Kimura
4) Sakata International Trading
Company
5) 1983(Japan)
1247 1) foundation(cultural
foundation)
2) Shigeshi Omori
3) Eiko Sakata
4) Suntory Cultural Foundation
5) 1979(Japan)
6) dark green(Pantone350c)
1248
2),3) PVDI
4) Serpro Service Federal de
Processamento de Dados
5) 1973(Brazil)
1249 1) conference
(transportation)
2),3) Velizar Petrov
4) Seminar on Problems of
European Transport
Infrastructure
5) 1983(Bulgaria)
6) green/ultramarine
1250 1) interior(furniture
production)
3) Marcello d'Andrea
4) P.L.Spagnolo
5) 1980(Italy)
6) red
1251 1) plastic industry
2) Joe Selame
3) Selame Design Group
4) Sterilite Plastic Co.
5) 1970(U.S.A.)
6) black/red
1252 1) construction material
2) Maurizio Milani/Armando
Milani
3) Maurizio Milani
4) Italver(Architectural Grass)
5) 1983(Milano)
1253 1) pharmacy
3) Miani Luigi
4) Salus Pharmacy
5) 1979(Milano)

6) red
1254 1) office
supply(manufacture)
2),3) Joseph Boggs
4) Eastern Systems,Inc.
5) 1974(U.S.A.)
6) red
1255 1) real estate
3) Florent Garnier
4) Semicle Immobilier
5) 1972(Lyon)
6) black
1256
2),3) Ettore Vitale
4) Snia Difesa e Spazio
5) 1981(Rome)
1257 1) athletic(training
program)
2),3) Scott Engen
4) Solitude Ski Team
5) 1983(U.S.A.)
6) black/red(PMS032)/
blue(PMSRef.)
1258 1) packing material shop
3) Yoshikatsu Tami
4) Sogien
5) 1976(Japan)
1259 1) leather(manufacture)
2),3) Hans E.Scheur
4) Segor Co.
5) 1977(West Germany)
6) red/black
1260 1) electric machinery and
appliance
2),3) Akisato Ueda
4) Seiwa Electric Co.,Ltd.
5) 1982(Japan)
1261 1) association(sporting
goods industry association)
2),3) Kazumasa Nagai
4) Japan Sporting Goods
Industry Association
5) 1975(Japan)
6) red
1262 1) printing
2),3) Robert Hargenhoffer
4) S.J.Surnamer Co.,Inc.
5) (U.S.A.)
1263 1) Supermarket
2) Jitsuo Hoashi
3) Hoashi Studios
4) The Seiyo Stores,Co.
5) 1974(New York)
6) red(PMS183)
1264 1) chemical
2),3) Kazuo Tanaka
4) Torii & Co.,Ltd.
5) 1983(Japan)
6) DIC221/DIC163
1265 1) sport(skiing area)
2),3) Alfredo de Santis
4) Sella Nevea
5) 1978(Rome)
1266
2),3) Adam Moltke
4) Sanistaal,Ltd.
5) 1981(Denmark)
6) dark blue
1267 1) festival(exhibition)
2),3) Felix Beltran
4) Galeria Uneac
5) 1970(Mexico)
6) black
1268 1) transport
2) Gottschalk+Ash

International
3) Stuart Ash
4) Sudbury Transit
5) 1972(Toronto)
1269 1) printing
3) Kazuharu Fujii
4) Sakamoto Printing Co.
5) 1977(Japan)
1270 1) sport(tennis club)
2),3) Katsunori Oda
4) Sun Square Tennis Club
5) 1979(Japan)
1271 1) publication
2),3) Shigeo Katsuoka
4) Chikuma Shobo Co./
Chikuma Seminar
5) 1983(Japan)
1272
2),3) Angelo Sganzerla
4) Schwarz
5) 1970(Rome)
6) black
1273 1) theatre
3) István Szekeres
4) Scenika PJT
5) 1982(Budapest)
6) blue
1274 1) graphic & industrial
design office
3) A.G.Schillemans
4) The Designer himself
5) 1970(Amsterdam)
6) dark blue
1275 1) bank
3) Carlo Malerba
4) Banca Del Sud
5) 1980(Italy)
6) blue
1276 1) bookstore
2),3) Jost Hochuli
4) Bookstore Sesam
5) 1974(Switzerland)
6) black
1277 1) bathing facility
2),3) Bror B.Zetterborg
4) Bathing Facilities Company
5) 1980(Helsinki)
6) brown
1278 1) chemical(sale)
2),3) Kazuo Tanaka
4) Shin Nihon Jitsugyo Co.,
Ltd.
5) 1970(Japan)
1279 1) textile printer
2),3) Othmar Motter
4) Johann Schwärzler
5) 1979(Austria)
6) black
1280 1) jewel
2),3) Paul Ibou
4) Sidar-Diamant(Antwerpen)
5) 1971(Belgium)
1281 1) painting
2),3) Eduardo A.Cánovas
4) Finobra S.A.
5) 1981(Buenos Aires)
6) red
1282 1) dyeing
2),3) Burton Kramer
4) Surfacing
5) 1981(Toronto)
6) purple
1283 1) steel
2),3) Victor Dicristo
4) Shankey Steel Supply

5) 1970(U.S.A.)
6) black
1284 1) design studio
2) Ricardo Salas
3) Javier de Leon
4) Tintas Sanchez Graphic Art
Inc.
5) 1981(Mexico)
6) gray/black
1285 1) computer
2),3) Morfos Diseño
4) Software International Inc.
5) 1978(Mexico)
6) gray
1286 1) building material(sale)
2),3) Shigeji Kobayashi
4) Goesu Industry Co.,Ltd.
5) 1981(Japan)
1287 1) real estate
2),3) Bob Swisher
4) Stafford-Corley Realtors
5) (U.S.A.)
6) red
1288 1) iron manufacture
2),3) Dicken Castro
4) Siderurgica Del Pacifico
-Sidelpa
5) 1976(Colombia)
1289
2),3) Paul Ibou
4) Suglo
5) 1973(Belgium)
1290 1) hotel
2),3) Katsumi Maetani
4) Hotel Sepias Muroran
5) 1983(Japan)
1291 1) research
institute(dental technique)
3) Toshiaki Takahasi
4) Showa Technical Institute
5) 1975(Japan)
1292 1) association(science)
2),3) Stan Brod
4) Cincinnati Science Center
5) 1970(U.S.A.)
6) red
1293 1) construction
2),3) Oanh Pham-Phu
4) Saumweber Stecher
5) 1974(München)
6) ocher
1294 1) festival(sculpture
festival)
2),3) Burton Kramer
4) Sculpture Festival
5) 1979(Toronto)
6) blue
1295 1) office
machine(manufacturer)
2),3) Burton Kramer
4) Storwal International
5) 1977(Toronto)
1296 1) industry
2),3) Kao Yu-Lin
4) New Style Industry Co.,Ltd.
5) 1979(Taipei)
6) red
1297 1) auto industry
2),3) Gustavo Gomez
-Casallas/Rodrigo Fernandez
4) Sincromotors
5) 1978(Colombia)
6) black/yellow
1298 1) textile industry
2),3) Oanh Pham-Phu

4) Ernst Schamong KG
5) 1972(München)
6) green
1299 1) spinning
2),3) Othmar Motter
4) Schöller-Gruppe,Zürich
5) 1976(Austria)
6) black
1300 1) cosmetic(soap)
2),3) Fumio Koyoda
4) Max Co.,Ltd.
5) 1983(Japan)
1301 1) picture gallery
2),3) Angelo Sganzerla
4) Spagnoli Gallery,Firenze
5) 1973(Rome)
6) black
1302
2),3) Don Davis
4) Synatron
5) 1972(U.S.A.)
6) black
1303 1) computer(systems)
2),3) Jorge Canales
4) Systematics De Mexico, Inc.
5) 1978(Mexico)
6) black/red
1304 1) industry(thermostats)
2) Jorge Canales
3) Jorge Canales/Fernando de
la Serna
4) Selas De Mexico, Inc.
5) 1982(Mexico)
6) orange(Pantone152)
1305
3) Tytus Walczak
4) Stoteczny Ośrodek
Sportowy
5) 1971(Warsaw)
6) black
1306 1) hospital
2),3) Robert Hargenhoffer
4) South Shore Mental Health
Center
5) (U.S.A.)
1307 1) blanket(manufacture)
2),3) Othmar Motter
4) Sannwald Co.
5) 1982(Austria)
6) black
1308 1) travel-agency
2),3) Manfred Wutke
4) Sinuhe,Travel-Agency(Cairo)
5) 1982(West Germany)
6) blue
1309 1) textile industry
2),3) Jorge Canales
4) Santiago Textil, Inc.
5) 1975(Mexico)
6) brown(Pantone160)
1310
2),3) Michael Herold
5) 1974(West Gremany)
6) yellow/red/blue
1311 1) publishing
2),3) Makoto Yoshida
4) Shimamura Shuppan Co.,
Ltd.
5) 1973(Japan)
6) blue
1312 1) electronic industry
2),3) Makoto Yoshida
4) Shimobe Denshi Co.,Ltd.
5) 1973(Japan)
6) dark navy blue

1313
2),3) Michael Herold
4) Stadt
5) 1983(West Germany)
6) blue/green
1314 1) construction
3) Matiaz Bertonceli
4) Staubar Maribor and Dos
5) 1974(Yugoslavia)
6) blue
1315 1) building
materials(manufacture),
2),3) Guastavo Gomez
-Casallas/Rodrigo Fernandez
4) Ladrillera Santafe
5) 1978(Colombia)
6) reddish brown
1316 1) airplane
parts(manufacture)
2) Thomas Ohmer
3) Lou Frimkess
4) Sierracin Corporation
5) 1971(Los Angeles)
1317 1) trade(wood)
2),3) Damien Harrington
4) Structural Softwoods, Ltd.
5) 1982(Ireland)
6) orange
1318 1) gallery(sculpture)
3) Shigeo Fukuda
4) Seiho-Sha
5) 1976(Japan)
1319 1) trade
2),3) Sudarshan Dheer
4) Style Asia Limited(Hong
Kong)
1980(Bombay)
6) silver
1320 1) diamond(manufacture
and trade)
2),3) Sudarshan Dheer
4) Shrenuj & Co.
5) 1976(Bombay)
6) purple
1321 1) society
2),3) Ettore Vitale
4) EPS:European Propulsion
Society
5) 1982(Rome)
1322 1) filter(manufacture)
2),3) Tor Pettersen
4) Stella Meta Filters
5) 1970(London)
6) black
1323 1) atomic energy
development industry
2),3) Giovanni Brunazzi
4) Sigen
5) 1975(Italy)
1324 1) printing
3) Carlo Malerba
4) Serit srl
5) 1977(Italy)
1325
3) Florent Garnier
4) Sigma Diffusion
5) 1980(Lyon)
6) silver
1326 1) vegetable and
fruit(retail store)
2),3) Akira Sanada
4) Tarami Seika(Shine Foods)
5) 1981(Japan)
1327 1) architectural design
firm

Index to Contained Works

2),3) Shintaro Ajioka
4) Taiyo First-Class
Architectural Firm
5) 1981(Japan)
1328 1) association(sporting
arms and ammunition
manufacturers association
2),3) Takenobu Igarashi
4) Japan Sporting Arms &
Ammunition Manufacturers
Association
5) 1974(Japan)
1329
2),3) Ernesto Lehfeld
4) Sales Stamps
5) 1973(Mexico)
6) PMS 132
1330 1) commercial affair
2),3) Yasuhisa Iguchi
4) Seiko Shoji
5) 1983(Japan)
1331
2),3) George Tscherny
4) Roto-Rooter
5) 1981(New York)
6) red or black
1332 1) solar heating
device(manufacture)
2),3) Silvio Coppola
4) Saim Solar
5) 1972(Italy)
1333 1) glass industry
2),3) Jorge Sposari
4) Soifer, Inc.
5) 1977(Buenos Aires)
6) green
1334 1) printing
2),3) Giovanni Brunazzi
4) Instituto Geografico de
Agostini
5) 1979(Italy)
1335 1) electronic industry
2),3) Arthur Eckstein
4) Struthers Electronics
Corporation
5) 1976(New York)
6) black
1336 1) design studio
2),3 Gerd Leufert
4) Estudio Uno
5) 1979(Venezuela
6) black
1337 1) printing
2),3) Hiroshi Manzen
4) Sun Art Printing Co.,Ltd.
5) 1983(Japan)
6) DIC 310
1338 1) chemical petroleum
industry
3) Fred E.Denzler
4) Sunnyside Corporation
5) 1970(U.S.A.)
6) black/ocher yellow
1339 1) foundation
(educational)
2),3) Edward Hughes
4) The Spencer Foundation
5)1973(U.S.A.)
1340 1) school
2),3) Burton Kramer
4) Project "School-To-School"
5) 1971(Toronto)
6) orange
1341
2),3) R.Roger Remington

4) Saratoga Performing Arts
5) 1975(New York)
6) blue(PMS 285U)
1342 1) sound
device(manufacture)
3) Pentti Ruuska
4) S.O.K.
5) 1975(Finland)
1343
2),3) Paul Ibou
4) Spaarkrediet(Antwerpen)
5) 1982(Belgium)
1344 1) broadcasting
(television program)
2),3) Yasuhisa Iguchi
4) TV Tokyo
5) 1983(Japan)
1345 1) private school for
learning
2),3) Yasuhisa Iguchi
4) Suginoko Academy
5) 1983(Japan)
6) green/red
1346 1) food(manufacture)
3) Ling Chay Y. Lao
4) Sols Chicken
5) 1983(Philippines)
6) gold
1347 1) construction
2),3) Chermayeff & Associates
4) Key Sabinal
5) (U.S.A.)
6) Black/white
1348 1) pottery(manufacture)
2),3) Philip J. Turner
4) Hornsea Pottery Co.,Ltd.
5) 1976(Great Britain)
1349 1) educational center(art)
2),3) F. R. Esteban
4) Sweetwater Arts Center
5) 1978(U.S.A.)
6) black
1350 1) supermarket
2) Joe Selame
3) Selame Design Group
4) Shaw's Supermarkets
5) 1973(U.S.A.)
6) green/orange
1351 1) commercial affair
2),3) Robert Hargenhoffer
4) Saxon Industries,Inc.
5) (U.S.A.)
1352
2),3) Adam Moltke
4) Schultz Shipbrokers
5) 1982(Denmark)
6) dark blue
1353 1) construction
2) Mike Quon/F. Cordero
3) Mike Quon
4) Specialty House,Inc.
5) 1978(New York)
6) red/orange
1354 1) construction(road)
3) Frutiger Adrian
4) Autoroute du Sud de la
France
5) 1975(France)
6) black
1355 1) private
symbol(photograher)
2),3) Tony Forster
4) Douglas Sargent
5) 1974(Manchester)
6) black

1356 1) festival(sport)
2) Shigeshi Omori
3) Eiko Sakata
4) Suntory
5) 1979(Japan)
6) dark blue(Pantone 282C)
1357 1) food(manufacture)
2),3) Cyril John Schlosser
4) Spencer Foods Inc.
5) 1971(U.S.A.)
6) red(PMS 185)
1358 1) sport(shop)
2),3) Gustavo Gomez
-Casallas/Rodrigo Fernandez
4) Stadium-Almacen De
Articulos Deportivos
5) 1977(Colombia)
6) red
1359 1) design studio(graphic)
2),3) Hugo Arape
4) Servicios Graficos
5) 1983(France)
6) brown
1360 1) metalworking industry
2) Ray Engle
3) Ben Lizardi
4) Supracote
5) 1972(U.S.A.)
6) blue/green/black
1361 1) welding equipment
3) Abram Games
4) ARO Welding Equipment
Co.
5) 1977(London)
6) blue
1362 1) teenager shop
2),3) Othmar Motter
4) Sigrid Amann
5) 1968(Austria)
6) black/white
1363
2),3) Don Davis
4) Scandia-Blair
5) 1972(U.S.A)
6) black
1364 1) medicine
2),3) Unger Erich
4) Steiner Pharmacy
5) 1982(West Berlin)
6) blue
1365 1) pottery(manufacture)
2) Elias Santamarina
3) José Santamarina
4) "San Claudio" Fabrica de
Loza
5) 1974(Spain)
6) black/maroon
1366 1) planning(display)
2),3) Takao Yoguchi
4) System Creates
5) 1978(Japan)
1367 1) construction
2),3) Ivan Dvoršak
4) Slovenija Ccste Tehnika and
Dos
5) 1979(Yugoslavia)
6) blue
1368 1) printing
2),3) Hans E.Scheur
4) Printer
5) 1972(West Germany)
6) dark blue
1369 1) society(skin science)
2),3) Jaime Gutierrez Lega
4) Colombia Society of Skin

Science
5) 1974(Colombia)
6) black
1370 1) printing
2) Ladislaus Popper
3) Gerd Leufert
4) Sistemas Drupo
5) 1975(Venezuela)
6) black
1371 1) real estate
2) Thomas Ohmer
3) Tom Wilson
4) Fred Sands Realty
5) 1976(Los Angeles)
6) brown/white
1372
2),3) Don Connelly
4) Specialty Graphics
5) 1977(U.S.A.)
6) blue
1373 1) publication(magazine
title)
2),3) Tetsuya Ota
4) Goma Shobo
5) 1978(Japan)
1374 1) religion(priest
retirement program)
2),3) Edward Hughes
4) Senior Jesuits Program
5) 1978(U.S.A.)
1375 1) food(manufacture)
2),3) Tadamasa Katsube
4) Marute Shokuhin
5) 1983(Japan)
1376 1) construction
(window/front door)
2),3) Othmar Motter
4) Seraphin Pümpel & Söhne
Co.
5) 1973(Austria)
6) black
1377
2),3) Jack Evans
4) Sterling Projects,Inc.
5) (U.S.A.)
1378 1) papermaking
3) Stanislav Kovář
4) Severomoravské
5) 1983(Prague)
6) blue
1379 1) printing
3) Jiří Rathouský
4) Bratislava Slovakian Printing
Industry
5) 1981(Czechoslovakia)
6) black
1380 1) cothing
2),3) Stephan Kantscheff
4) Boyan Chonos Vidin
5) 1974(Canada)
6) red
1381
2),3) John S.Brown
4) The Safety Supply Company
5) 1974(Canada)
6) red
1382
2),3) Hans Kündig
4) Säto Produicter AB Uppsala
5) 1978(Sweden)
6) black
1383 1) bank
2),3) James Lienhart
4) State Bank of Slinger
5) (U.S.A.)

1384 1) machine industry
2),3) Kao Yu-Lin
4) Sye-Hsing Machinery Mfg. Co.
5) 1978(Taipei)
6) red
1385 1) school
2),3) Marty Neumeier
4) Summit University
5) 1974(U.S.A.)
6) black
1386 1) publishing(magazine)
2),3) James Lienhart
4) Savings Institutions
5) 1983(Chicago)
1387 1) lease
2),3) Manfred Korten
4) Systema Leasing Ltd.,Köln
5) 1978(West Germany)
6) black
1388
2),3) Tamás Ernö
4) Szolidaritás
5) 1983(Budapest)
6) blue
1389
2),3) Tamás Ernö
4) Szövorg
5) 1982(Budapest)
6) dark brown
1390 1) construction
2),3) Terry Lesniewicz/Al Navarre
4) SBS Construction Management
5) 1980(U.S.A.)
1391 1) publicity(propaganda)
2),3) Claudio Doveri
4) Studio Doveri
5) 1983(Milano)
1392 1) publication
2),3) Félix Beltrán
4) Signos
5) 1972(Mexico)
6) black/or other colors
1393 1) telephone
2),3) Giovanni Brunazzi
4) SIP
5) 1975(Italy)
1394 1) petroleum
2),3) Paul Ibou
4) SNE -petroleummij(Antwerpen)
5) 1970(Belgium)
1395 1) food(technical development)
2) Tadashi Ishikawa
3) Hideko Sakato
4) Shin Nihon Shokken
5) 1981(Japan)
1396 1) wrought iron industry
2) Stankowski/Duschek
3) Anton Stankowski
4) Söll
5) 1970(West Germany)
1397 1) advertisement
2),3) Giancarlo Iliprandi
4) Societá Pubblická Eolitoriale
5) 1982(Milano)
6) dark blue
1398 1) restaurant(enterprise)
2) Shigeshi Omori
3) Eiko Sakata
4) Suntory Restaurant System
5) 1983(Japan)

6) orange(Pantone warm red)
1399 1) design studio
3) Yutaka Sato
4) Sun Sano Sogei-Sha
5) 1982(Japan)
1400 1) food(manufacture)
2) Dave Bartells
3) Gale William Ikola
4) Sunstar Foods,Inc.
5) 1973(U.S.A.)
6) red/orange
1401 1) advertisement agency
2),3) Takeshi Ootaka
4) Soft System 21
5) 1982(Japan)
1402 1) guild(dress making)
2),3) Akisato Ueda
4) Super Tailors Club
5) 1973(Japan)
1403 1) private symbol(architect)
3) Nikola Nikolov
4) Snejana Terzieva
5) 1982(Bulgaria)
6) black/white
1404 1) art museum
2),3) Kazumasa Nagai
4) Tokyo Central Museum
5) 1971(Japan)
6) blue
1405 1) commercial affairs
2) Ishine Nituma
3) Taijiro Nakayama
4) Taichi Shoji
5) 1981(Japan)
1406 1) radiator(manufacturer)
2) Paolo Gotti
3) Maurizio Osti
4) Termocalor
5) 1975/1977(Italy)
6) brown
1407 1) interior(furniture manufacture)
2) Ove Engström
3) Ove Engström/Eva-Lotta Fruhoff
4) Trivás
5) 1982(Sweden)
6) black/red
1408 1) architectural design firm
2) Takenobu Igarashi
3) Takenobu Igarahi/Akinori Nagao
4) Taniguchi,Takamiya, & Assoc
5) 1980(Japan)
1409 1) watch(manufacture)
2) Ove Engström
3) Kurt Karlsson/Ove Engström
4) Bestime
5) 1983(Sweden)
6) black/gray
1410 1) telephone
2),3) Henry Steiner
4) Hong Kong Telophone Co., Ltd.
5) 1978(Hong Kong)
6) orange
1411 1) school
2),3) Edward Hughes
4) Triton College
5) 1978(U.S.A.)
6) red
1412 1) private symbol
2) John Follis
3) Jean-Claude Müller

4) Tom Tramel
5) 1977(Los Angeles)
6) black/brown
1413 1) trade
2) Armando Milani/Maurizio Milani
3) Maurizio Milani
4) Top Export
5) 1981(Italy)
1414 1) broadcasting (television radio)
2),3) Stephan Kantscheff
4) Television Radio Committee
5) 1972(Bulgaria)
1415 1) society
3) Tytus Walczak
4) Stowarzyszenie Tkumaczy Polskich
5) 1979(Warsaw)
6) black
1416 1) school(technical school)
2),3) Jean-Claude Müller
4) Technicum de Stlmier
5) 1974(U.S.A.)
6) black
1417 1) pottery manufacture
3) Kazuharu Fujii
4) Tachibanayaki Seitosho
5) 1981(Japan)
1418 1) bank
3) Shigeo Fukuda
4) Tokyo Tomin Bank
5) 1976(Japan)
1419 1) maker of camping
2),3) Walter Hergenröther
4) Calegari & Ghigi
5) 1970(Italy)
6) blue/green/orange/black
1420 1) theatre
2),3) Felix Beltran
4) Teatro la Tertulia
5) 1972(Mexico)
6) deep blue
1421 1) leather(manufacture)
2),3) Maurizio Milani/ Armando Milani
4) Trombi Francesca
5) 1980(Milano)
1422 1) industry(heat)
2),3) Eduardo A.Cánovas
4) Termac Industries
5) 1979(Argentina)
6) brown
1423
2) Ove Engström/Torgny Gustavsson
4) Alucrome Corrosion Treatment Co.
5) 1981(Sweden)
6) blue/gray
1424 1) gallery
2) Yonefusa Yamada
3) Shin Sasaki
4) Gallery Mimi
5) 1978(Japan)
1425 1) design studio
2),3) Shuji Torigoe
4) Torigoe Design Co.,Ltd.
5) 1979(Japan)
6) blue(DIC183)
1426 1) industry(technical)
2) Thomas Ohmer
3) Koji Takei
4) Tower Industries,Inc.

5) 1981(Los Angeles)
6) silver
1427 1) real estate
3) Sumio Hasegawa
4) Takuso
5) 1980(Japan)
1428 1) museum
3) Jiří Rathouský
4) National Technical Museum
5) 1978(Czechoslovakia)
6) various colors or black
1429 1) body(protection of laborers)
2),3) Felix Beltran
4) Ministerio del Trabajo
5) 1970(Mexico)
6) blue
1430 1) fishing gear
2),3) Koichi Watanabe
4) Taiheiyo Marine Co.,Ltd.
5) 1981(Japan)
1431 1) business firm
2) Burton Kramer
3) Joe Gault/Burton Kramer
4) Trade Typesetting
5) 1976(Toronto)
6) burgundy/red
1432 1) construction
2),3) Morfos Diseño Co.
4) Tilysa,Construcciones
5) 1980(Mexico)
6) burgandy
1433 1) hospital
2) Tadamasa Katsube
3) Kenji Sakamoto
4) Takeuchi Iin
5) 1978(Japan)
1434 1) construction
2),3) Shigenobu Nagaishi
4) Toyofuku-Kensetsu
5) 1981(Japan)
1435 1) nightclub
2),3) Teruo Fujishige
4) Tanigawa Jitsugyo
5) 1974(Japan)
1436 1) interior(furniture manufacture)
2) R.Nava/G.Romani/D. Soffientini/A.Ubertazzi
3) Environmental Design Center
4) Tornaghi Mobiliere
5) 1979(Italy)
6) cyclahmen-colored
1437 1) construction
2) R.Nava/G.Romani/D. Soffientini/A.Ubertazzi
3) Environmental Design Center
4) Tecnostampi
5) 1977(Italy)
6) green
1438 1) design studio
2),3) Takenobu Igarashi
4) Takenobu Igarashi Design Firm
5) 1975(Japan)
1439 1) iron manufacture
2),3) Marchionni Carlo
4) Resehini Emzo/Corri Donia
5) 1977(Italy)
6) red/orange/black
1440 1) society(bulletin)
2),3) Takenobu Igarashi
4) Japan Typography

Association
5) 1978(Japan)
1441 1) advertisement
2) Shizuo Yoneda
3) Koichi Watanabe
4) Tate Co.,Ltd.
5) 1982(Japan)
1442 1) haberdashery
2),3) Yasaburo Kuwayama
4) Tenguya
5) 1979(Japan)
6) purple
1443 1) interior(design)
2),3) Shigenobu Nagaishi
4) Tanaka Sohshoku
5) 1983(Japan)
1444 1) textile industry
3) Rosmarie Tissi
4) Teamtex
5) 1976(Zürich)
6) black
1445
2),3) Denise Spaulding
4) Ostech
5) 1983(U.S.A.)
6) red/gray
1446 1) broadcasting
(television network)
2),3) Alfredo de Santis
4) Teleconfronto
5) 1983(Rome)
1447 1) jeweller
3) Paul Ibou
4) Tache Diamons
5) 1973(Belgium)
1448 1) publication
2),3) Stephan Kantscheff
4) Publishing House Technica
5) 1980(Bulgaria)
1449 1) transport
2),3) Felix Beltran
4) Ministerio de Transporte
5) 1970(Mexico)
6) black
1450
2),3) Ettore Vitale
4) Tecnolyte
5) 1971(Rome)
1451 1) leather(manufacture)
3) Judita Skalar
4) Toko
5) 1979(Yugoslavia)
6) brown
1452 1) private symbol
3) Chris Brand
4) private
5) (Netherlands)
1453 1) construction
2),3) John M.Alexander
4) Tucker Construction
5) 1983(U.S.A.)
6) blue
1454 1) transport
3) Velizar Petrov
4) National Transport Complex
5) 1978(Bulgaria)
1455
2),3) Silvio Coppola
4) Toluian
5) 1971(Milano)
1456 1) specialty store
building
3) Shigeo Fukuda
4) Tenzin Core
5) 1976(Japan)

1457 1) hotel
3) Assen Ivanov
4) Hotel "Trimontium"
5) 1979(Bulgaria)
6) brown
1458 1) office supplies(sale)
2),3) Othmar Motter
4) Kurt Thurnher
6) black/white
1459
2),3) Tamás Ernö
4) Tokaj Áruház
5) 1983(Budapest)
6) orange/red
1460
3) Michael Herold
4) Theissen Inc.
5) 1980(West Germany)
6) blue
1461 1) committee(sight
-seeing)
2),3) Allan W.Miller
4) Tijuana Tourism Committee
5) 1976(U.S.A.)
6) purplish red
1462 1) local center
2),3) Burton Kramer
4) Tillsonburg Town Centre
5) 1980(Toronto)
6) orange
1463 1) contracting business
2),3) Don Connelly
4) T & B Scottdale Contractors
5) 1983(U.S.A.)
1464 1) communication
3) Peter Dabinett
4) Bord Telecom Eireann
5) 1980(Ireland)
6) blue
1465 1) research institute
3) Velizar Petrov
4) Institute for Ergonomy and
Organization of Labour
5) 1983(Bulgaria)
6) blue
1466 1) foundation
2),3) George Tscherny
4) Trust Funds
5) 1981(New York)
6) black or red(Pantone172)
1467
2),3) Keith Murgatroyd
4) Tom Green Ltd.
5) 1982(London)
6) green
1468 1) private
symbol(married couple)
3) Yutaka Sato
4) Tadayuki Tsutsui and
Harumi Tsutsui
5) 1978(Japan)
1469
2) Léderer Károly
3) Ernö Sára
4) Transinvest
5) 1982(Budapest)
6) dark green/red
1470 1) travel agency
2),3) Gustavo Gomez
-Casallas/Rodrigo Fernandez
4) Turismo Hubenil America
5) 1978(Colombia)
6) yellow/ocher
1471 1) private
symbol(married couple)

3) Yutaka Sato
4) Toshio Yasui and Kimie
Yasui
5) 1979(Japan)
1472
2),3) Arnold Saks
4) Time-Life
5) 1969(New York)
6) red
1473 1) broadcasting
(television production)
2),3) Eita Shinohara
4) Three Mast
5) 1987(Japan)
1474 1) measurement industry
2),3) Yasuhisa Iguchi
4) Toyo Keisoku
5) 1982(Japan)
1475
2) William Carson
3) Douglas Williams
4) Tommy Matusi, Inc.
5) 1977(U.S.A.)
6) ocher
1476
3) Carlo Malerba
4) Tecnomarmi
5) 1979(Italy)
6) black
1477 1) textile industry
2),3) Selahattin Sönmez
4) Özhamurkar Tekstil
5) 1978(Istanbul)
6) blue
1478 1) publication
2),3) Stephan Kantscheff
4) Targowsko Obsa Weshdane
5) 1973(Bulgaria)
1479 1) printing
2),3) Yukihisa Takakita
4) Totani Insasu
5) 1979(Japan)
1480 1) advertisement
3) Nikola Nikolov
4) Bulgarian TV
5) 1980-81(Bulgaria)
6) black/white
1481 1) medical
instrument(sale)
3) Hiroyasu Saijo
4) Therapy Co.,Ltd.
5) 1981(Japan)
1482 1) education(device)
2) Keith Murgatroyd
3) Keith Murgatroyed/Tony
Forster
4) Tequipment Ltd.
5) 1976(Manchester)
1976(London)
6) orange/black
1483 1) heavy industry
2) Jorge Canales
3) Jorge Canales/Fernando
De Serna
4) Tecfril
5) 1982(Mexico)
6) green(Pantone341)
1484 1) metal(standard)
2),3) Félix Beltrán
4) Tecnotec
5) 1980(Cuba)
6) gray
1485 1) school(technical
school)
2),3) Jean-Clude Müller

4) Technicum De Stlmier
5) 1974(U.S.A.)
6) black
1486 1) association(bank)
2),3) Don Connelly
4) Georgia Bankers Association
5) 1980(U.S.A.)
6) green
1487
2),3) Ed Penniman
4) Taylorvision Sathellite Dishes
5) 1983(U.S.A.)
6) PMS192/PMS109/
PMS368
1488 1) design studio
2),3) Tetsuya Ohta
4) Tetsuya Ohta Design Studio
5) 1980(Japan)
1489 1) electric
appliance(manufacture)
2),3) Kao Yu-Lin
4) Tatung Co.
5) 1978(Taipei)
6) black
1490 1) leisure(building)
2),3) Shintaro Ajioka
4) Tack
5) 1977(Japan)
1491 1) theatre
2),3) Gustavo Gomez
-Casallas/Rodrigo Fernandez
4) Teatro Popular De Bogota
5) 1979(Colombia)
6) dark blue
1492 1) foundation(theatre)
2),3) Charles Fuhrman
4) Theatre Development Fund
5) 1980(U.S.A.)
1493 1) printing
2),3) Cyril John Schlosser
4) Type House+Duragraph
Inc.
5) 1982(U.S.A.)
6) blue(PMS293)
1494 1) trade
3) Miani Luigi
4) Iron Trade International
5) 1978(Milano)
6) blue
1495 1) interior
2),3) Stephan Kantscheff
4) Stad Tschirpan
5) 1972(Bulgaria)
1496 1) textile industry
2),3) Stephan Kantscheff
4) Top
5) 1982(Bulgaria)
1497 1) theater
2),3) Rinaldo Cutini
4) Teatro Popolare di Roma
5) 1975(Rome)
6) dark red
1498 1) Packing
2) Akiteru Nakajima
3) Kumi Shirahama
4) Toyo Packaging Corp.
5) 1983(Japan)
1499 1) trade
2),3) Azar Khosrovi-Ivorsohk
4) Traders International
5) 1979(New York)
6) blue(Pantone301)
1500
2),3) Gale William Ikola
4) Investors Diversified

Services,Inc.
5) 1977(U.S.A.)
6) brown
1501 1) textile industry
2),3) Stephan Kantscheff
4) Tonsos
5) 1971(Bulgaria)
1502 1) air conditioning
equipment industry
2),3) Monica Morales
4) Turbocompresores Inc.
5) 1981(Mexico)
6) brown(Pantone483)／
orane(Pantone158)
1503 1) metal industry
2),3) Matiaž Bertonceli／Ivan
Dvoršak
4) TVT Boris Kidrič
5) 1982(Yugoslavia)
6) black／silver／green
1504 1) food(manufacture)
2),3) Dicken Castro
4) Tecnicaña
5) 1978(Colombia)
6) green
1505 1) business firm(hygiene)
3) Ivan Dvoršak
4) Tosama-Domžale
5) 1977(Yugoslavia)
6) blue
1506 1) guarantee
2) Christensen Peter
3) Burkhalter Marc
4) Pavatex
5) 1982(Switzerland)
6) black
1507
2),3) Don Davis
4) Touvel Corp.
5) 1978(U.S.A.)
6) purple／black
1508
2),3) Silvio Coppola
4) Tessitura Di Giussano
5) 1970(Milano)
1509 1) broadcasting
(television station)
2),3) Alfredo De Santis
4) RAI
5) 1971(Rome)
1510
2),3) Joe Sondrman
4) The Hilton Head Company
5) 1972(U.S.A.)
6) gold
1511
3) Frutiger Adrian
4) Traduction Oecumenique de
la Bible
5) 1974(France)
6) black
1512 1) theatre
2),3) Claude Dieterich
4) TUC
5) 1977(Peru)
1513 1) airline
2) Saul Bass
3) Saul Bass／Herb Yaeger and
Assoc.
4) United Airlines
5) 1974(Los Angeles)
6) blue／red
1514
2),3) Maurizio Millani
4) Ulshore

5) 1981(Milano)
1515 1) school
3) Ivan Dvoršak
4) Mariboru University
5) 1977(Yugoslavia)
1516 1) association(aluminum
industry)
2),3) Ivan Dvoršak
4) Unial, Maribor
5) 1979(Yugoslavia)
6) silver
1517 1) club(giving help in
case of traffic accidents
2),3) Manfred Korten
4) Unfallhife Wuppertal Club
5) 1975(West Germany)
6) black
1518
2),3) Michael Herold
5) 1976(West Germany)
6) blue／brown
1519 1) household
articles(manufacturer)
2),3) Michio Ogura
4) Umebachi Kogyo
5) 1976(Japan)
1520 1) music(record)
2),3) Hugo Arape
4) Uraniun Records
5) 1983(Venezuela)
1521 1) committee
(universiade)
2) Joji Tanaka
3) Shigo Yamaguchi
4) Kobe Universiade Executive
Committee
5) 1982(Japan)
1522
2),3) Paul Ibou
4) Unirep
5) 1970(Belgium)
1523
2) Philip Gips
3) Philip Gips／Gina Stone
4) United Satellite Communica
5) 1983(New York)
1524 1) storage company(bulk
liquid storage)
3) Kenneth Hollick
4) Unitank Storage Company
5) 1976(London)
6) blue／white
1525 1) research
institute(energy)
2),3) Michael Richards
4) Office of Energy
Coordination, University of
Utah
5) 1974(U.S.A.)
6) orange
1526 1) construction(express
highway)
2),3) Nicolay Pecareff
4) Ingstroi Highway
Constructors
5) 1982(Bulgaria)
6) black／yellow
1527 1) building
material(cement industry)
2),3) Giovanni Burnazzi
4) Unicem
5) 1975(Italy)
6) gray／black
1528 1) mechanical
industry(grain treatment)

2),3) Fernando Rión
4) Ultramag
5) 1974(Mexico)
6) red
1529
3) Ivan Dvoršak
4) Univerzitetna Knjižnìca
Maribor
5) 1983-84(Yugoslavia)
6) black
1530
2),3) Ettore Vitale
4) Unione Italiana di
Riassicurazione
5) 1978(Roma)
1531
2) Armando Milani／Maurizio
Milani
3) Maurizio Milani
4) Unione Fornitori Cancelleria
5) 1980(Milan)
1532 1) association
2),3) Robert Hargenhoffer
5) (U.S.A.)
1533 1) insurance
2),3) Chermayeff & Geismar
Associates
4) La Universal
5) (U.S.A.)
1534 1) hospital
2),3) Eduardo A. Cánovas
4) Urologic Surgery Center
5) 1979(Buenos Aires)
6) black／red／blue／yellow
1535 1) construction
2),3) George Delany
4) Urban Design Group
5) 1975(U.S.A.)
6) Gray／black
1536 1) restaurant
2),3) Milton Glaser
4) The Underground Gourmet
5) 1966(New York)
6) black／pink／orange
1537 1) boutique(accessories)
2) Akira Hirata
3) Hiroshi Tada
4) Yuai Co.,Ltd.
5) 1977(Japan)
6) Pantone 147C
1538 1) design studio
2),3) Yuji Baba
4) Uni Design Co.,Ltd.
5) 1971(Japan)
1539 1) alcoholic
drink(manufacture)
2) John DiGianni
3) Giannonoto Associates, Inc.
4) Vinicola Vergel, Inc.
5) 1977(U.S.A.)
6) various colors
1540 1) multi-industry
enterprise
2),3) João Carlos Cauduro／
Ludovico Antonio Martino
4) Indústrias Villares, Inc.
5) 1970(São Paulo)
1541 1) automobile
2),3) Conrad E. Angone
4) Vito's Italian Cars
5) 1976(Los Angeles)
6) red／green
1542 1) construction
2),3) Felix Beltran
4) Vargas, Inc.

5) 1976(Mexico)
6) gray
1543 1) publication
2),3) Félix Beltrán
4) Instituto del Libro
5) 1971(Cuba)
1544 1) medical instrument
2),3) Martrlossi Giobanni
4) Ven Hospital
5) 1974(Milan)
6) blue
1545 1) boutique
2),3) Othmar Motter
4) Boutique Veronika
5) 1980(Austria)
1546 1) clothing(ladies'
clothing
2),3) Othmar Motter
4) Vanessa Ladies' Clothing
5) 1979(Austria)
1547 1) textile industry
2),3) Othmar Motter
4) Die vorarlberger Textil
-Industrie
5) 1982(Austria)
6) black
1548 1) bicycle industry
2) Christensen Peter
3) Wicki Robert
4) Villiger Söhne
5) 1980(Switzerland)
1549 1) sound device
2) George Mcginnis
4) Voicemasters, Inc.
5) 1982(New York)
1550 1) design studio
2),3) Nagato Kawamoto
4) Visual Communications
5) 1979(Japan)
1551 1) clothing
2) Shakespear Design Studio
3) Raul Shakespear & Ronald
Shakespear
4) Vega Men's Clothing
5) 1977(Buenos Aires)
6) blue
1552 1) welfare
2),3) Victor Dicristo
4) Milwakee Advertising Club
Volunteers
5) 1973(U.S.A.)
6) black
1553 1) park
2),3) Jack Evans
4) Valwood Park
5) (U.S.A.)
1554 1) bank
2),3) Everett Forbes
4) Virginia Beach Bank of
Commerce
5) 1977(U.S.A.)
6) blue
1555
2) Petar Naumov
3) Nicolay Pecareff
4) Vassyl Levsky's Regional
Administration For Education
5) 1982(Bulgaria)
6) blue
1556
3) Florent Garnier
4) Peintures Vachon
5) 1971(Lyons)
6) red
1557 1) real estate

2),3) Tetsuo Noda
4) Nichimo Prefabrication
5) 1973(Japan)
1558 1) business of carrying passengers
2),3) Elias Garcia Benavides
4) Trenes Vertebrados
5)1974(Spain)
6) Silver
1559 1) society(savings & loan)
2),3) Gerd Leufert
4) La Vivienda
5) 1977 (Venezuela)
6) black
1560
2),3) Silvio Coppola
4) Vide
5) 1978(Milan)
1561 1) interior(retail)
2),3) George Delany
4) Verlaine, Inc.
5) 1983(U.S.A.)
6) burgundy/gold
1562 1) investment company
2),3) Ben Bos
4) Vedior Investments
5) 1976(Amsterdam)
6) blue
1563 1) association (management)
2),3) Rey Dacosta R.
4) Vayo & Associates
5) 1974(Venezuela)
6) purple(30%)
1564 1) glass industry
2),3) Francesco Burcini
4) Vetreria Angelana
5) 1981(Italy)
6) green/light green
1565 1) printing
2),3) Paul Ibou
4) Van Baarle Press
5) 1970(Belgium)
1566 1) sport(football games)
2),3) Ron Richards
4) Canadian University Football Championship
5) 1982(Toronto)
6) purple/gold
1567
3) Taijiro Nakayama
4) Verde Japan
5) 1983(Japan)
1568
2),3) Chermayeff & Geismar Associates
4) Veeder-Root, Inc.
5) (U.S.A.)
6) black/white
1569 1) plastic industry(toy)
3) Szekeres, István
4) Vör-Sas
5) 1979(Budapest)
1570 1) educational center(audiovisual)
2),3) Eita Shinohara
4) Audiovisual Scientific Technical Center
5) 1975(Japan)
1571
2),3) Paul Ibou
4) Vlaams Ekonomisch Verbond(Antwerpen)
5) 1980(Belgium)
1572 1) video

software(production)
2),3) Shigo Yamaguchi
4) Vis Inc.
5) 1983(Japan)
1573
2),3) Michael Herold
5) 1981(West Germany)
6) blue
1574
2),3) Paul Ibou
4) V.K.W.
5) 1982(Belgium)
1575 1) travel agency
2),3) Steve Shelden
4) Van Nuys Travel
5) 1981(U.S.A.)
6) black
1576 1) mechanical industry
2),3) Francesco Burcini
4) Volpi
5) 1976(Italy)
6) gray/red
1577 1) photograph(studio)
2),3) James Lienhart
4) Von Photographer
5) (Chicago)
1578 1) construction(studio)
2),3) Jack Evans
4) Vantage Planning Systems Architectural Service
5) (U.S.A.)
1579 1) publication
2),3) Joseph Enterprises
5) 1978(U.S.A.)
6) blue(PMS 279)
1580 1) insurance
2) Keith Murgatroyd
3) Tony Forster
4) Walmsleys Insurance, Ltd.
5) 1981(Manchester)
6) gold/dark blue
1581
2) Kenneth R. Cooke
3) Robert Wolf
4) Weatherford International, Inc.
5) (New York)
1582
2),3) Silvio Coppola
4) Parmalat
5) 1978(Milan)
1583 1) sport(uniform)
2),3) Yoshimichi Morioka
4) Taiyo Corporation professional baseball team
5) 1973(Japan)
6) DIC 221
1584
2),3) Milton Glaser
4) Grand Union Company
5) 1979(New York)
6) black/red
1585 1) automobile manufacturing plant(racing car)
2),3) Sogen Onishi
4) West Racing Cars Co.,Ltd.
5) 1983(Japan)
1586 1) local self-governing body(ladies)
3) Kenzo Takashima
4) Toyama Prefecture
5) 1981(Japan)
6) green/red
1587 1) movie · publication · record

2) Saul Bass
3) Saul Bass/Herb Yaeger and Assoc.
4) Warner Communications
5) 1974(Los Angeles)
1588 1) metallurgical industry
2),3) Heinz Waibl
4) Smalteria Metalurgica
5) 1973(Milan)
1589 1) real estate
2),3) H. W. Lohman
4) Werim
5) 1978(Holland)
6) PMS 165/black
1590 1) publication
2),3) Herbert Wenn
4) Scientific Books publishing House
5) 1976(West Germany
6) red
1591 1) clothing store(jeans)
2),3) Eduardo A. Cánovas
4) J. Charrúa
5) 1971(Argentina)
6) black/gold
1592 1) work(public)
2),3) Joe Sonderman
4) Ralph Whitehead & Assoc.
5) 1975(U.S.A.)
6) various colors
1593 1) clothing
2),3) Diana Graham
4) Wings Shirt Co.
5) 1982(New York)
6) black
1594 1) construction
2),3) Conrad E. Angone
4) Wamsley Construction Co.
5) 1975(Los Angeles)
6) green
1595
2) Kazimieiz Mann
3) Jarostaw Jasinski
4) W.S.Inwalidow
5) 1972(Warsaw)
6) black
1596
2),3) Carl Nelson
4) Welsh Companies,Inc.
5) 1981(U.S.A.)
6) black/rust color(PMS 159)
1597 1) lighting(sales)
2),3) Ray Engle
4) Wood Lighting Industries
5) 1982(Los Angeles)
6) black/yellow
1598 1) convenience store
2) Hiromi Kuginuki
3) Akira Hirata/Koji Mori
4) Wellmart Co.,Ltd.
5) 1982(Japan)
1599
2),3) Peter G. Ulmer
4) Wanner AG Baggerunternehmen
5) 1981(Switzerland)
6) green
1600 1) fountain pen(manufacturer)
2) Yvette & Roland Michau
3) Rudi Meyer
4) Waterman Co.
5) 1983(Paris)
6) blue/yellow
1601 1) beauty parlor

2),3) Yasaburo Kuwayama
4) Watanabe Beauty Parlor
5) 1983(Japan)
6) brown
1602 1) real estate
2),3) Ray Engle
4) Westaire Properties
5) 1971(Los Angeles)
6) blue/black
1603 1) shopping center
2),3) Robert P. Gersin
4) Taubman
5) 1971(New York)
6) red
1604 1) studio
2),3) Yasuo Wada
4) Atorie Zokan
5) 1983(Japan)
1605 1) clothing store
2),3) Harry Murphy
4) Upper Stuff
5) 1969-70(U.S.A.)
6) black/white
1606 1) brewing and distilling
2),3) Othmar Motter
4) Wieser-Bräu
5) 1982(Austria)
6) black/white
1607 1) sport(tennis club)
2),3) Ken'ichi Hirose
4) Tennis Club With
5) 1982(Japan)
6) blue
1608 1) interior(furniture manufacturer)
2),3) Oanh Pham-Phu
5) 1975(München)
6) brown
1609
2),3) George Tscherny
4) Weidlinger Associates
5) 1983(New York)
6) black/tint of black(40%)
1610 1) construction
2),3) Francesco Burcini
4) 1972(Italy)
6) brown
1611 1) private symbol(photographer)
2),3) Herbert Wenn
4) Wolfgang Mirbach
5) 1982(West Germany)
6) black/white
1612 1) private symbol(exhibition designer)
2),3) Tony Forster
4) Gordon McWilliams
5) 1974(Manchester)
6) silver
1613
2),3) Bill Bundzak
4) Weather Routing, Inc.
5) 1978(New York)
6) blue
1614 1) clothing(manufacture)
2),3) Hagihara Co.,Ltd.
5) 1977(Japan)
1615 1) Mark for construction car
2),3) Yasaburo Kuwayama
4) Watchtower Bible and Tract Society
5) 1970(Japan)
6) black/white
1616 1) building

material(manufacture and sale)
2),3) Takeo Sugaya
4) Towa Shoko,Limited
5) 1982(Japan)
1617 1) construction
2),3) Ray Engle
4) Widom Wein & Partners
5) 1979(Los Angeles)
6) silver/blue
1618 1) medicine
2),3) Marty Neumeier
4) Western Medical, Ltd.
5) 1975(U.S.A.)
6) tan
1619 1) fiberglass
(manufacturer)
2),3) Terry Lesniewicz/Al
Navarre
4) Owens-Corning Fiberglass
Corporation
5) 1983(U.S.A.)
1620 1) association(woman
movment)
2) Joe Selame
4) The League of Women
Voters of Massachusetts
5) 1971(U.S.A.)
6) blue/gold
1621 1) type(manufacturer)
2),3) Gert Wunderlich
4) Bayerische Letter
5) 1979(East Germany)
6) black
1622 1) publication(magazine)
2),3) Masakazu Tanabe
4) X Magazine
5) 1982(Japan)
1623 1) shop(stamp)
2),3) Felix Beltran
4) Xellos, Havana
6) gray
1624 1) bank
2) Henry Steiner
3) Henry Steiner/G. Di
Bondone
4) Hongkong Bank
5) 1983(Hong Kong)
6) red
1625
2),3) George Tscherny
4) Design Built Exhibits
5) (New York)
1626 1) educational center
2),3) PVDI
4) Xerox Educational Center
5) 1971(Brazil)
1627 1) exhibition
2),3) Félix Beltrán
4) Xpos
5) 1970(Cuba)
6) black
1628
2),3) Keith Murgatroyd
4) Culter Guard Bridge, Ltd.
5) 1972(London)
6) red/purple
1629 1) exhibition
2),3) Carlo Malerba
4) Expostand
5) 1980(Italy)
1630 1) congress(fur dressing)
2),3) Velizar Petrov
4) 10th Fur-Dressing
International Congress
5) 1982(Bulgaria)

6) gold
1631 1) exchange shop
2),3) Michael Vanderbyl
4) Yachtmen's Exchange
5) 1974(U.S.A.)
6) dark blue
1632
2),3) Los Shakespear
5) (Buenos Aires)
1633
2),3) Stephan Kantscheff
4) Chlebna
5) 1972(Bulgaria)
1634 1) sport(competition)
2),3) Tchakarov Stefan
4) 1982 European basketball
championship
5) 1982(Bulgaria)
6) black/white
1635 1) camera
2),3) Tadasu Fukano
4) Canon Sales Co.,Inc.
5) 1975(Japan)
1636 1) mechanical industry
2),3) Stan Krol
4) W. E. Norton
5) 1970(London)
6) black
1637 1) construction
2),3) Dicken Castro
4) Sociedad Colombiana de
Arquitectos
5) 1974(Colombia)
1638 1) bank
2),3) Kazumasa Nagai
4) Yasuda Trust Bank
5) 1974(Japan)
6) blue
1639 1) public agency
2),3) Damien Harrington
4) Youth Employment Agency
5) 1982(Ireland)]
6) green
1640 1) construction
2),3) Burton Kramer
4) Ytong Construction
5) 1970(Toronto)
1641 1) construction
2),3) Burton Kramer
4) York Construction
5) 1972 (Toronto)
6) red
1642 1) market
3) Michael Herold
4) Stuttgarter Messe Und
Kongress GMBH
5) 1979(West Germany)
6) blue
1643 1) agency
3) Paul Ibou
4) Tolimpex(tolagentschap)
5) 1977(Belgium)
1644
2),3) Paul Ibou
4) Scientific Research
Valuation Center
5) 1981(Belgium)
1645
2) Gottschalk+Ash
International
3) Stuart Ash
4) York Center
5) 1973(Toronto)
1646 1) leather(manufacture)
2),3) Shigeji Kobayashi

4) Yamaura Co.,Ltd.
5) 1980(Japan)
1647 1) plumbing
implement(sales)
2),3) Kazumasa Nagai
4) Yamane Works, Ltd.
5) 1973(Japan)
6) blue
1648
2) Ichiro Okada
3) Koichi Watanabe
4) Yanagi Co.,Ltd.
5) 1976(Japan)
1649 1) interior(shop)
2),3) Koichi Watababe
4) Yoshino Interior
5) 1976(Japan)
1650 1) store
2),3) Stephan Kantscheff
4) Universal Store
5) 1980(Bulgaria)
1651 1) pottery(manufacture)
2),3) Stephan Kantscheff
4) USPEC
5) 1972(Bulgaria)
1652 1) design studio
2) Iwao Yamaguchi
3) Yamachan Planning
5) 1979(Japan)
1653 1) fiber
2),3) Akisato Ueda
4) Yamada Co.,Ltd.
5) 1974(Japan)
1654 1) festival('83 TGC
exhibition, points of contact
between people and science)
2),3) Kiyoshi Kyoi
4) Tokyo Graphic Designers
Club
5) 1983(Japan)
1655 1) beauty culture
3) Masaaki Ishii
4) Yuasa Beauty Parlor
5) 1977(Japan)
1656 1) design studio
2),3) Yonefusa Yamada
4) Yamada Design Room
5) 1968(Japan)
1657 1) photograph(DPE)
2),3) Yonefusa Yamada
4) Yoshioka photograph studio
5) 1980
1658 1) private
symbol(designer)
2),3) Hidemichi Yamao
4) Yamao Design Office
5) 1983(Japan)
6) Pantone104c
1659 1) union organization
2),3) Franktišek Boban
5) 1976(Czechoslovakia)
1660
2) Masayuki Nishizawa
3) Hiroshi Iseya
4) Yamamoto Balster Co.,Ltd.
5) 1983
1661 1) private
symbol(married couple)
3) Yutaka Sato
4) Yutaka and Hideko Sato
5) 1980(Japan)
1662 1) clothing
2),3) Stephan Kantscheff
4) Tchaika Dimitrowgrad
5) 1974(Bulgaria)

1663 1) leather dyeing business
2) Kuniharu Masubuchi
3) Ikuo Masubuchi
4) Yamaura Senkaku
5) 1980(Japan)
1664 1) type(manufacture)
2),3) Gert Wunderlich
4) Bayerische Letter
5) 1979(East Germany)
1665 1) industry
2),3) PVDI
4) Zillo Industry
5) 1972(Brazil)
1666
2) Armando Milani/Maurizio
Milani
4) Armando Milani
5) Zerowatt
5) 1977(Milano)
1667 1) stationery(fountain
pens)
2) Mitsuo Ishida
3) Tetsuhiro Tateshi
4) Platinum Fountain Pen
5) 1980(Japan)
1668 1) pottery manufacture
2),3) Eduardo A.Cánovas
4) Cerámica Zanon
5) 1978(Argentina)
6) green/red
1669 1) paint shop
2),3) Ken Eichenbaum
4) Zummach Paint Company
5) 1970(U.S.A.)
6) blue/red/yellow/black
1670 1) consultant(finances)
2),3) James Lienhart
4) Zeisler & Associates,Inc.
5) (Chicago)
1671 1) heating device
2),3) Rudi Meyer
4) Zaegel Held
5) 1979(France)
6) green/yellow
1672 2),3) Stephan Kantscheff
4) Staats Mühlen
5) 1970(Bulgaria)
1673 2),3) Michael Herold
5) 1981(West Germany)
6) yellow/red
1674 1) environmental
design(firm)
2),3) Takenobu Igarashi
4) Zen Environmental Design
5) 1974(Japan)
1675 1) construction
2),3) Tony Foster
4) Zenex
5) 1981(Manchester)
6) gray
1676 1) restaurant
2),3) Stan Brod
4) Zion's Restaurant
5) 1980(U.S.A.)
6) dark green
1677 1) private symbol
2),3) Kazuo Ono
4) Yoko Nyui
5) 1981(Japan)
1678 1) academic
society(economic research)
3) Miloš Ćirić
4) Zavod Za Ekonokske
5) 1981(Belgrade)
6) blue

Index to Category of Business

association (union/academic society/ conference)
1,23,27,40,52,62,65,67,104,123,156,218,249,282,298, 300,315,365,412,433,434,483,533,535,536,551,699,703, 704,743,765,787,792,793,883,923,926,930,980,1048, 1050,1071,1077,1085,1090,1126,1144,1145,1179,1199,1201, 1247,1249,1292,1321,1328,1369,1402,1415,1429,1440,1461, 1486,1517,1521,1532,1559,1563,1620,1630,1659,1678

public agency (government/self-governing body/assembly/research institute)
13,237,360,389,403,428,434,448,451,452,471,472,474, 475,513,700,707,857,882,898,945,949,956,987,1026, 1056,1065,1088,1114,1291,1465,1525,1552,1586,1639

park
1553

foundation
79,411,489,493,708,1339,1466,1492

agriculture/foresty/fisheries (gardening)
70,494,576,653,710,751,1156,1184,1232

industry
59,91,157,215,252,256,274,342,394,485,522,606,720, 963,983,1013,1296,1304,1426,1483,1655

mechanical industry
120,121,139,152,161,257,312,349,359,484,511,550,638, 676,823,969,1001,1080,1119,1206,1316,1322,1361,1384, 1406,1474,1528,1541,1548,1576,1636,1647

automobile
53,80,89,306,325,527,529,682,768,821,993,1051,1218, 1230,1237,1297,1541,1585

electrical machinery and appliances
17,57,95,98,213,229,362,392,442,453,455,490,548,561, 626,728,885,903,912,1015,1107,1216,1260,1332,1489, 1502,1597,1671

chemical industry
31,103,163,260,297,310,314,416,419,464,555,1160,1282, 1338,1669

steel (metal)
28,279,350,421,649,663,683,709,721,773,846,915,931, 976,978,1098,1235,1243,1283,1288,1360,1396,1439,1484, 1503,1588,1621,1664

petroleum
338,497,706,940,1025,1099,1111,1394

plastic
572,832,897,1035,1127,1244,1251,1569

glass
107,220,247,436,642,1333,1564,1619

fiber (textile/clothing)
2,11,46,160,188,221,227,231,234,340,377,420,441,499, 506,521,533,594,600,637,731,746,749,777,790,816,841,

856,888,892,911,919,924,934,955,1038,1162,1164,1183, 1245,1279,1298,1299,1307,1309,1380,1442,1444,1477, 1496,1501,1537,1539,1545,1546,1547,1551,1591,1593,1605, 1614,1653,1662

leather (boots and shoes/bag)
378,426,869,1176,1259,1421,1451,1646,1663

electronic industry (computer)
21,106,111,266,319,353,458,481,482,512,598,690,732, 828,905,913,1086,1093,1285,1303,1312,1335

construction (building material/ public works)
9,20,30,41,134,169,170,172,212,214,222,242,259,303, 317,330,334,335,337,379,380,385,396,399,405,492, 495,503,524,554,568,588,610,612,640,643,650,666,679, 689,691,730,835,874,921,947,950,959,977,991,1036, 1052,1066,1106,1132,1154,1161,1217,1224,1236,1240,1252, 1281,1286,1293,1315,1322,1347,1353,1354,1367,1376, 1377,1432,1437,1453,1468,1526,1527,1535,1542,1578, 1592,1594,1610,1616,1617,1637,1640,1675

engineering
450,466,654

light and heat (energy)
26,78,99,174,422,652,1147,1233,1323,1422

art/curio/pottery (ceramic)
16,180,541,844,881,899,1029,1348,1365,1417,1651,1668

interior design
66,88,93,124,147,155,164,182,203,216,228,285,293,356, 397,480,562,618,641,654,659,669,671,687,724,739,772, 783,831,839,937,995,1010,1016,1068,1151,1159,1173,1177, 1250,1407,1436,1443,1495,1561,1608,1649

stationery/office supplies
109,210,275,609,952,975,1254,1295,1458,1600,1667

toy
829

food
131,192,200,239,250,321,375,410,417,491,651,705,715, 747,748,763,795,796,860,927,999,1043,1067,1128,1157, 1326,1346,1357,1375,1395,1400,1504

alcoholic drink
635,1539,1606

confectionry
602

drink (tea)
948

product manufacture
130,153,246,265,367,583,1211

business firm (trade)
32,101,284,299,496,518,711,767,776,929,1084,1246,1317, 1319,1330,1351,1405,1413,1431,1494,1499,1505

circulation of money (bank/credit union)
3,116,142,145,189,197,205,209,211,223,224,226,233,254, 277,292,294,347,460,470,488,519,549,698,702,824,

836,868,875,917,990,1018,1039,1101,1122,1196,1223,1275, 1383,1418,1554,1624,1631,1638

real estate/housing
18,39,42,355,361,592,723,764,928,951,970,1021,1031, 1045,1060,1082,1103,1124,1140,1255,1371,1427,1557,1589, 1602

precious metals (jewel/accessories)
331,429,680,734,737,815,962,1130,1150,1171,1280,1320, 1447

education/cultural facilities (school/ library)
14,24,29,63,84,90,125,190,240,251,273,276,352,357, 363,364,395,423,461,479,520,593,697,755,760,825, 834,837,910,960,1000,1005,1008,1148,1208,1345,1349, 1385,1411,1416,1485,1515,1570,1626

museum (art gallery)
336,808,851,908,938,946,982,996,1034,1197,1404,1428, 1627,1629

religion (temple/church)
69,238,1089,1374,1615

hospital
158,193,201,264,445,543,577,578,579,601,623,667,681, 788,810,848,1070,1165,1209,1306,1433,1534

chemical (medicine)
1158,1202,1253,1264,1278,1364,1618

medical care (instrument)
909,968,1481,1544

beauty parlor (barbershop)
859,941,986,1073,1601,1655

cosmetics
48,73,346,559,647,992,994,1300

daily necessities/favorite
487,502,586,713,766,822,827,843,997,1227,1409,1519, 1597,1635

leasing
8,510,589,692,1095,1387

consultants
196,391,515,604,657,811,845,1221,1670

seach/planning/development/ design (accountant)
47,76,110,794,818,935,1024,1100,1104,1110,1182,1190, 1222,1327,1408,1674

investment/bill (stock holdings/ stockbroking/settlement of mortgage)
96,313,324,381,383,458,500,540,563,684,693,757,778, 780,972,1238,1562

insurance (guarantee)
624,964,1178,1195,1506,1533,1580

department store (supermarket/ shopping center)
55,68,108,136,165,178,219,262,278,414,447,476,557,

625,629,762,769,785,791,805,958,1042,1059,1061,1233,
1263,1350,1362,1456,1598,1603,1623,1642,1650

eating house (restaurant/tea house)
36,159,384,457,565,581,774,879,902,1063,1152,1398,
1435,1536,1676

hotel (inn)
296,327,444,614,619,630,631,660,907,973,1044,1112,
1137,1155,1290,1457

movie/drama (theater)
83,311,351,406,415,427,575,896,1047,1054,1120,1273,
1420,1491,1497,1512,1587

music (sound apparants)
77,181,301,478,531,537,580,587,596,729,801,833,847,
942,1040,1094,1104,1113,1143,1169,1214,1342,1520,1549,
1587

recreation center (zoo/botanical garden)
1133,1135,1165,1490

sport
6,547,570,608,622,670,673,750,849,852,871,900,957,
1017,1028,1053,1064,1134,1149,1205,1210,1231,1257,1265,
1270,1358,1419,1566,1582,1607,1634

photography (photo studio)
248,271,322,348,509,521,542,716,756,761,782,865,1136,
1219,1577,1657

printing/paper (packaging material)
7,38,118,126,138,151,166,210,241,253,258,270,409,440,
462,516,545,617,648,672,674,675,694,725,726,733,754,
789,814,858,880,1002,1012,1033,1083,1102,1105,1123,
1174,1187,1189,1191,1194,1225,1262,1269,1324,1334,1337,
1370,1378,1379,1479,1493,1498,1565

publication (bookstore)
15,25,49,61,71,74,100,162,167,177,191,208,408,424,425,
446,449,467,507,509,521,558,585,799,840,877,890,914,
918,933,939,943,1007,1032,1079,1167,1204,1239,1271,
1276,1311,1373,1386,1392,1448,1478,1543,1579,1587,
1590,1622

news (broadcasting newspaper)
51,105,288,343,344,370,544,677,718,800,826,895,989,
1153,1344,1414,1446,1473,1509,1572

communication (mail/telephone)
645,1393,1410,1464

transport (flight/ship)
44,82,87,146,267,430,486,498,501,523,728,759,881,891,
925,985,1020,1041,1046,1096,1081,1116,1268,1430,1449,
1454,1513,1558

advertisement (advertisement agency)
10,86,133,173,243,269,332,345,508,597,615,714,758,
781,812,819,884,971,1006,1391,1397,1401,1441,1480

travel (travel agency)
60,154,283,295,366,463,584,678,742,817,887,889,1004,
1308,1470,1575

resort
35,712

service industry
72,75,132,135,143,183,198,456,517,861,922,998,1215

gallery (painting material)
199,245,326,591,611,853,893,944,953,998,1170,1301,
1318,1424,1604

design studio
34,50,64,119,137,144,176,194,255,318,368,374,388,393,
400,413,468,514,533,613,685,701,740,803,804,806,1014,
1030,1069,1087,1139,1185,1203,1220,1228,1274,1284,
1336,1359,1399,1425,1438,1488,1538,1550,1652,1656

campaign (festival/exhibition)
19,22,112,140,184,207,230,323,328,358,387,407,469,
532,534,539,566,695,744,894,954,984,1118,1166,1193,
1212,1267,1294,1356,1654

private symbol
54,81,94,128,171,217,236,305,401,404,530,567,590,599,
616,656,736,745,752,775,786,802,838,961,1186,1226,
1355,1403,1412,1452,1468,1471,1612,1658,1661,1677

Yasaburo Kuwayama (About the Editor)

Yasaburo Kuwayama was born in Niigata prefecture, Japan in 1938. He graduated from the Musashino Art University in 1962 and taught typography at Asagaya Academie des Beaux-arts for five years from 1966. In 1969, he established the Kuwayama Design Room. In 1970, he began teaching typography at the Musashino Art university. In 1972, he began serving as an [Examiner of Lettering]. In 1975, he began teaching lettering at the Asahi Culture Center and served as a permanent manager of the Japan Creative Finish Work Association. In 1979, he retired from his posts in : the Musashino Art University, The Organization of Lettering Approval, the Asahi Culture Center, and the Japan Creative Finish Work Association. His retirement from these posts enabled him to create moretime for other interests. At present, he is a member of the Association du Typographique Internationale (A. TYP. I), the Japan Typography Association (JTA), the Federation of German Typographers (BOB), the Tokyo Designers Space (TDS), and the Japan Graphic Designer Association (JAGDA). He is a member of the Jehovah Witness Christian faith. His main books include "Lettering & Design", "Typeface Design" and "Graphic Elements of The World."

Editor : Yasaburo Kuwayama／Publisher : Kashiwashobo

1985-1991 Works Being Solicited
Marks, Symbols, Logotypes, Pictograms, Signs, Typefaces

Many marks, symbols, logotypes, pictograms and typefaces are designed every year, but what is the role that they play ? In order to find an answer to this question, marks, symbols, logotypes, pictograms, signs and typefaces are being solicited from designers for publication in a book.

Instead of just a record of works, this book will provide abundant material for reference in design, in searching for similar works, and in research. Since publication of an international edition is being planned, this book will undoubtedly benefit design circles throughout the world.

●Works Solicited
1. Marks, Symbols
2. Logotypes
3. Pictograms, Signs
4. Typefaces
5. Below you'll find instructions for application to the above mentioned categories.
   * Attach a photograph to works used in a special way or which develop in a special way. For example, those which change or move.
   * Specify special points.

●Period Works designed and used from 1985 to 1991
* Includes works redesigned during this period

●Size
1. Marks, Symbols :   about 4 cm
2. Logotypes :   about 9 cm
3. Pictograms, Signs :   about 3 cm
4. Typefaces :   Height of one word about 2 cm
   * Other sizes are acceptable.
   * Paste the work on the application slip.
   * When submitting color photographs please use positive film. If black and white film, please send 5×7" prints.
   * Printed matter can be submitted.
   * For works that you want returned, write "R" in red.
   * Attach application slips to examples of the designer's work.
   * In cases where pictograms, signs and typefaces make up sets, paste the works on pasteboard and an application slip on the pasteboard.

●Category Circle one of the following :
1. Marks, symbols
2. Logotypes
3. Pictograms, Signs
4. Typefaces

●Points to be Noted
1. Motif or Production Aim (less than 30 words)
2. Business Category
3. Name of the Art Director(s)
4. Name of the Designer(s) (including colleagues)
5. Client
6. Year and Place Designed
7. Color (attach color samples or color proofs)
   * Write in English as much as possible
   * When writing by hand, please write clearly

●Deadline March 1, 1992

●Send to Kuwayama Design Room
1-3-1-501 Higashi Izumi, Komae-shi, Tokyo 201, Japan
   * Ask for or make copies if you want more application slips.
   * No application charge is required, but payment will not be made for works submitted.

* Works will not be returned (color positives will be returned).
* Some works may not be included in the book due to editing considerations.
* There are no qualifications or restrictions on the number of works submitted.
  The following works cannot be included in the book.
* Works already included in this series.
* Works with no application slip attached or with inadequate entries on the application slip.
* Works which are inadequate as block copy.

Editor Yasaburo Kuwayama
Member, Japan Typography Association (JTA)
Member, International Typography Association (ATYPI)
Member, Japan Graphic Designers Association (JAGDA)
Member, Tokyo Designers Space (TDS)
Special Member, BDB of West Germany

Publisher Kashiwashobo
1-13-14 Honkomagome, Bunkyo-ku, Tokyo 113
Tel (03) 947-8254

Book Size A4, about 480 pages, 3 to 5 volumes Publication
Date approximately April 1989

Paste Monochrome Work

Application Slip

Circle one of following: 1.Mark, Symbol 2.Logotype 3.Pictogram 4.Typeface

1. Motif or production aim

2. Business Category(or Use Contents)

3. Art Director

4. Designer

5. Client

6. Year and Place Designed

7. Color

* On reverse side, fill applicant's name, address and phone number.